complete Cocktails

the perfect drink for every occasion

R&R PUBLICATIONS MARKETING PTY LTD

Published by:
R&R Publications Marketing Pty Ltd
12 Edward Street
Brunswick Victoria 3056,
Australia
Phone: (61 3) 9381 2199
Fax: (61 3) 9381 2689
Australia wide toll free 1 800 063 296
E-mail: info@randrpublications.com.au
Web: www.randrpublications.com.au

Complete Cocktails

Publisher: Richard Carroll
Mixed Drinks Research: Jon Carroll
Graphic Designer: Elain Wei Voon Loh
Project Manager: Anthony Carroll
Photography: Warren Webb, Elain Wei Voon Loh, Anthony Carroll
Stylists: Marc Phillips, Alex Reed
Proofreader: LoftCom

ISBN: 1 74022 251 2
This edition printed February 2006
Computer Typeset in Din, Piranesi
Printed in China by Max Production Printing Ltd.

List of sponsors as follows:
The Publishers would like to thank and acknowledge the following companies for the supply of ingredients used in the making of relevant cocktails.

- **Phillip Lazarus (Agent for Libbey Glass of America)** – Suppliers of a wide rage of glassware to the retail and hospitality trade.
- **Cadbury-Schweppes Pty. Ltd.** – Suppliers of sparkling drink mixers.
- **Carlton & United Beverages** – Suppliers of Continental Liqueurs, SKYY Vodka and many other fine spirits and liqueurs.
- **Maxxium (Aust) Pty. Ltd.** – Absolute Vodka, Galliano, Cointreau, Grant's Scotch Whisky, Glenfiddich Malt Whisky.
- **Suntory (Aust) Pty. Ltd.** – Suppliers of Midori Melon Liqueur, Rubis Strawberry Liqueur, Mohala Mango Liqueur, Lena Banana Liqueur, Frangelico, Cuervo Tequila, Tullamore Dew Irish Whiskey, Opal Nera Sambuca, Jagermeister, Chambord, Chartreuse.
- **Alpen Products Pty. Ltd.** – Suppliers of novelties, decorations and swizzle sticks.

Contents

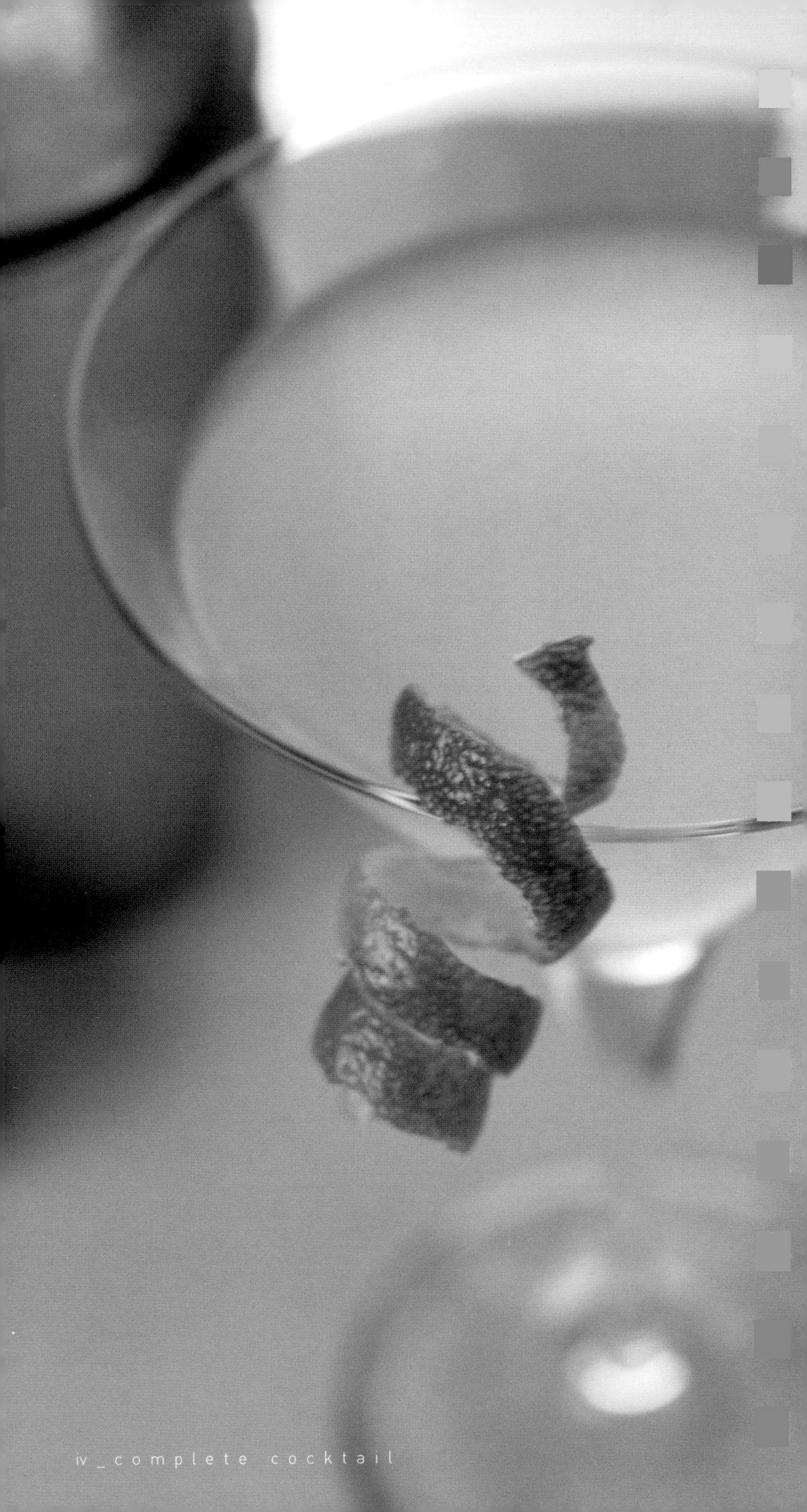

Introduction

HOW TO MIX COCKTAILS

1. Shake and strain

To shake is to mix a cocktail by shaking it in a cocktail shaker by hand. Shakers make it easy and practical to mix ingredients that do not combine easily with spirits, e.g. juices, egg whites, cream and sugar syrups.

Most shakers have two or three parts. First, fill the main part of the shaker three-quarters full with ice, then pour the ingredients on top of the ice. Less expensive ingredients should be poured before the deluxe ingredients. Shake vigorously for ten to fifteen seconds. Remove the cap or top part of the shaker and, using a Hawthorn strainer, the shaker's own built-in strainer or a knife, strain contents into the cocktail glass. This technique prevents the ice going into the glass, protecting the cocktail and ensuring melted ice won't dilute the flavour and mixture.

If you misplace the shaker cap, a coaster or the inside palm of your hand is quite effective. To sample the cocktail before serving to the customer, pour a small amount into the shaker cap and use a straw to check the taste.

2. Shake and pour

After shaking the cocktail as above, pour the contents straight into the glass, without straining out the ice. This technique is used when pouring into Hi-Ball glasses and sometimes old fashioned spirit glasses.

3. Stir and strain

To stir a cocktail is to mix the ingredients by stirring them with ice in a mixing glass and then straining them into a chilled cocktail glass. The stirring motion should be in short circular twirls. Spirits, liqueurs and vermouths that blend easily together are mixed by this method.

4. Build

To build a cocktail is to mix the ingredients in the glass in which the cocktail is to be served, pouring one on top of the other. Hi-Ball, long fruit juice and carbonated mixed cocktails are typically built using this technique. The drink should be served with a swizzle stick so that the customer can stir the ingredients. Long straws are excellent substitutes when swizzle sticks are unavailable.

5. Blend and pour

To blend a cocktail is to mix the ingredients using an electric blender or mixer. Any fruit (either fresh or tinned) should ideally be added first. Adding the fruit in small pieces gives a smoother texture than if you add the fruit whole. Next add the alcohol. Ice should always be added last. This order ensures that the fruit is blended thoroughly with the alcoholic ingredients before the ice chills the beverage.

Ideally, the blender should be on for at least 20 seconds, in order to prevent ice and fruit lumps forming that will need to be strained out. If the blender starts to rattle or hum, ice may be obstructing the blades.

Always check that the blender is clean before you start. Angostura Bitters is suitable for cleaning as it is ammonia based. Add 4 to 5 shakes to blender, fill with hot water, rinse and then wipe clean.

6. Layer or float

Layering or floating is done with ingredients that you do not want to blend with other ingredients. To do it, hold a bar spoon or dessert spoon the right way up and rest it with the lip slightly above the level of the last layer. Fill spoon gently and the contents will flow smoothly from all around the rim. Experienced bartenders use the back of the spoon.

7. Muddle

Muddling is the process of crushing or bruising fruit or mint garnishes in a glass with the muddler end of the bar spoon or with a pestle, often with some sugar and a small amount of liqueur. Other ingredients of the cocktail are added after muddling is complete. The muddling process extracts the maximum flavour from the fruit or mint. The drink can be strained after muddling if desired.

Introduction

PRESENTATION, BASIC RECIPES AND HINTS

1. Garnishing

Cocktail mixing is an art which is expressed in the preparation and presentation of the cocktail.

Simplicity is the most important fact to keep in mind when garnishing cocktails. Do not overdo the garnish: make it striking, but if you can't get near the cocktail to drink it, then you have failed. Many world-class cocktails are served simply with a slice of lemon, a twist of orange rind, or a single red cherry. Tall refreshing Hi-Balls tend to have more garnish as the glass is larger. Plastic animals, umbrellas, fans and a whole variety of novelty goods are now available to garnish with, and they add a lot of fun to the drink.

Long cocktails should usually be served with a swizzle stick for additional mixing. It's customary to serve straws both with highly garnished cocktails and with cocktails made for women to avoid lipstick rubbing off on the glass.

2. Frosting

Frosting with either salt or sugar is used both to decorate glass rims and mint leaves for garnishing. To frost a glass rim, first rub a lemon or orange slice around the rim until coated with juice. Lemon is used for salt-frosting and orange for sugar. Next, holding the glass by the stem, place the rim on a plate containing salt or sugar and turn slightly so that the salt/sugar adheres to the glass. Pressing the glass too deeply into the salt or sugar will result in chunks sticking to the glass.

To achieve colour effects with sugar-frosted glasses, coat the rim of the glass with a small amount of grenadine or coloured liqueur and then gently rub it in the sugar. The grenadine will absorb the sugar and turn it pink.

To frost mint leaves for garnish, dip leaves in water or egg white and then lay both sides on a saucer of caster sugar.

3. How to make a decorative cross

First, take two short straws and, with a sharp knife, slice one of the straws halfway through in the middle and wedge the uncut straw into the cut straw to create a cross. Lie this cross gently over the cocktail surface while dusting with nutmeg or other sprinkles. Remove the straw cross to reveal a blank cross pattern left on the surface. This can be used for creamy cocktails such as Brandy Alexanders.

4. Sugar syrup

Sugar syrup is needed in a good cocktail bar as sugar will not dissolve easily in cold cocktails.

To make the syrup, fill a cup or bowl (depending on how much you need) with white sugar. Top up the receptacle with boiling water until just about full, and keep stirring until the sugar is fully dissolved. Refrigerate when not in use. Keeps indefinitely.

5. Sour mix

Sour mix, is also known as bar mix, is an important part of many cocktails. To make sour mix, whisk one egg white until frothy in medium-sized bowl. Mix in 1 cup of sugar, then 2 cups of water and 2 cups of lemon juice. Beat until all the sugar is dissolved. The egg whites are optional, but will make the drinks slightly foamy. Will keep in refrigerator for about a week.

6. Handling fruit juices

Never leave juices, coconut cream or other ingredients in cans. Pour them into clean bottles, cap them and refrigerate them.

Empty 750mL glass spirit bottles make great storage bottles for fruit juices as you can attach a nip or free pourer to make it easier to pour the correct measurements. Before using the bottle, soak it in hot water to remove both the label and the flavour of the alcohol.

All the fruit cocktail recipes in this book have been tested using Berri fruit juices.

7. Handling ice

Ice is a vital ingredient of most cocktails and must be clean and fresh at all times. Small squared cubes and flat chips of ice are better for chilling and mixing cocktails. Ice cubes with holes are inefficient. Wet ice, ice scraps and broken ice should only be used in blenders.

To crush ice, fold the required amount of ice into a clean linen cloth and smash it against a solid surface. Although slightly uncivilised, this is an effective method. Don't use a bottle to hit the ice as this may shatter the bottle.

Alternatively, a blender may be used to crush ice. Half fill blender with ice and then pour in water until it reaches the level of the ice. Blend for about 30 seconds, strain out the water and you will have perfectly crushed ice. The blenders used to test these recipes were Moulinex blenders with glass jugs, which are of excellent quality. Portable ice crushers can also be purchased from some outlets.

Always use a scoop to collect the ice from an ice tray or bucket. Never pick up ice with your hands, as this is unhygienic. Shovelling a glass into an ice tray to gather ice can cause the glass to break and should be avoided.

It is important that the ice tray or bucket has been wiped clean before you put any ice into it, to ensure that the ice is kept clean.

1. Essential equipment

- BARSPOON/MUDDLER OR PESTLE
- BLENDER, ELECTRIC
- BOTTLE OPENERS
- CAN OPENER
- COASTERS AND NAPKINS
- COCKTAIL SHAKER
- CORKSCREW AND BOTTLE OPENER OR WAITER'S FRIEND
- FREE POURERS
- HAND CLOTHS FOR CLEANING GLASSES
- HAWTHORN STRAINER
- ICE BUCKET OR TRAY
- ICE SCOOP
- KNIFE, CUTTING BOARD
- MEASURES (JIGGERS)
- MIXING GLASS
- SCOOPER SPOON (LONG TEASPOON)
- SWIZZLE STICKS, STRAWS

2. Glasses – helpful hints

You can serve cocktails in any type of glass, but the better, cleaner, and more sparkling the glass, the better the appearance of the cocktail. Don't use scratched, marked or coloured glasses as they will spoil the appearance of the cocktail.

A good method to polish clean glasses is to hold each glass individually over a bucket of boiling water until the glass becomes steamy. Then rub the glass in a circular motion with a clean linen cloth until the glass is polished and gleaming. If the glass has a stem, hold it there while polishing to avoid marking the bowl of the glass.

All cocktail glasses should be kept chilled in a refrigerator or filled with ice while you are preparing the cocktails. An appealing effect on a glass can be achieved by running the glass under cold water and then placing it in the freezer.

All types of glasses have been designed for a specific type of drink, e.g.

- Hi-Ball glasses for long cool refreshing drinks.
- Cocktail glasses for novelty drinks.
- Champagne saucers for creamy after-dinner style drinks.
- Spirit glasses and tumblers for classic mixed drinks.
- Shot glasses for short strong drinks that are drunk in one hit (shooting).

3. Types of glasses

BEER MUG	355mL
BRANDY BALLOON	650mL
CHAMPAGNE FLUTE	140mL, 180mL
CHAMPAGNE SAUCER	140mL
COCKTAIL GLASS	90mL, 140mL, 220mL
CORDIAL GLASS (EMBASSY)	30mL
CORDIAL GLASS (LEXINGTON)	37mL
CORDIAL GLASS (TALL DUTCH)	45mL
FANCY COCKTAIL GLASS	210mL, 300mL
FANCY HI-BALL GLASS	220mL, 350mL, 470mL
FIESTA GRANDE GLASS	350mL, 490mL
FOOTED PILSENER GLASS	300mL
FOOTED HI-BALL GLASS	270mL, 300mL
HI-BALL GLASS	270mL, 285mL, 330mL
HURRICANE GLASS	230mL, 440mL, 650mL
IRISH COFFEE GLASS	250mL
MARGARITA GLASS	140mL, 350mL
MARTINI GLASS	90mL, 115mL, 145mL, 225mL, 275mL, 300mL
OLD FASHIONED SPIRIT GLASS	185mL, 210mL, 290mL
POCO GRANDE GLASS	380mL
PRISM ROCKS GLASS	270mL
SALUD GRANDE GLASS	290mL
SHOT GLASS	45mL
WINE GLASS	140mL, 190mL

4. Juices, garnishes and other ingredients

ALMONDS, SLIVERED
APPLE
APRICOT JAM
BANANA
BLUEBERRIES
CARBONATED WATERS
CELERY
CELERY SALT
CHOCOLATE FLAKES
CINNAMON
COCKTAIL ONIONS, RED

COCONUT CREAM
CREAM, FRESH, SINGLE AND WHIPPED
CUCUMBER
EGGS, FRESH
FLOWERS, ASSORTED PLASTIC
FRUIT NECTAR, CANNED
FRUIT PULPS, CANNED
FRUIT, CANNED
JELLY BABIES
LEMON JUICE, PURE
LEMONS
LIMES
MARASCHINO CHERRIES, RED
MILK, FRESH
MINT LEAVES
NUTMEG
OLIVES
ONIONS
ORANGE AND MANGO JUICE
ORANGES
PEPPER
PINEAPPLE, FRESH
PINEAPPLE, CRUSHED CANNED
ROCKMELON
SALT
STRAWBERRIES
SUGAR AND SUGAR CUBES
SUGAR SYRUP
TABASCO SAUCE
TOMATOES
VANILLA ICE CREAM
WORCESTERSHIRE SAUCE

5. Recommended spirits

- BRANDY
- CAMPARI
- GIN
- MALIBU
- OUZO
- PERNOD
- RUM, DARK AND LIGHT, E.G. BACARDI
- SOUTHERN COMFORT
- TEQUILA
- VODKA
- WHISKY, E.G. SCOTCH WHISKY, IRISH WHISKEY, CANADIAN CLUB WHISKY, TENNESSEE WHISKEY, BOURBON
- VANDERMINT

6. Recommended Vermouth

- VERMOUTH BIANCO
- VERMOUTH DRY
- VERMOUTH ROSSO

7. Recommended liqueurs

- ADVOCAAT
- AMARETTO
- BAILEYS IRISH CREAM
- BANANA LIQUEUR (LENA)
- BENEDICTINE
- CURAÇAO BLUE
- CASSIS
- CHARTREUSE, GREEN AND YELLOW
- CHERRY ADVOCAAT
- CHERRY BRANDY
- CLAYTON'S TONIC (NON-ALCOHOLIC)
- COCONUT LIQUEUR
- COINTREAU
- CRÈME DE CAFÉ
- CRÈME DE MENTHE GREEN
- CRÈME DE CACAO DARK
- DRAMBUIE
- FRANGELICO
- GALLIANO
- GRAND MARNIER
- GRENADINE CORDIAL (NON-ALCOHOLIC)
- KAHLÚA
- KIRSCH
- MANGO LIQUEUR (MOHALA)
- MELON LIQUEUR (MIDORI)
- ORANGE LIQUEUR
- PEACH LIQUEUR
- PIMM'S NO. 1 CUP
- SAMBUCA BLACK
- SAMBUCA CLEAR
- STRAWBERRY LIQUEUR (RUBIS)
- TIA MARIA
- TRIPLE SEC (WHITE CURAÇAO)
- VANDERMINT

Introduction

GLOSSARY OF LIQUEURS AND SPIRITS

ABSOLUT CITRON: A lemon-flavoured vodka.

ABSOLUT KURANT: A blackcurrant-flavoured vodka.

ADVOCAAT: A combination of fresh egg yolks, sugar, brandy, vanilla and spirit. Recommended shelf life is only 12–15 months from manufacture.

AMARETTO: A subtle liqueur with a distinct almond flavour. Amaretto (di Galliano) is a well-known brand.

AMER PICON: A bitter liqueur made with orange peel, quinine, spices and herbs. It is often used as a digestive.

AMONTILLADO SHERRY: A smooth-bodied sherry, golden-brown in colour, and aged in oak casks to give it a mellow nutty flavour.

ANGOSTURA BITTERS: An essential part of any bar or kitchen. A unique flavouring whose origins date back to 1824. A secret blend of natural herbs and spices, used as a flavouring agent in both sweet and savoury dishes and drinks. Ideal for dieters as it is low in sodium and calories.

ANISETTE LIQUEUR: A liqueur flavoured with anise oil.

APRICOT BRANDY: An apricot-flavoured liqueur.

AQUAVIT: A Scandinavian liquor with the flavour of caraway seeds.

ARMAGNAC: A brandy made in the demarcated region of Armagnac, France.

GLOSSARY OF LIQUEURS AND SPIRITS

ARRACK: A spirit distilled from the fermented sap of toddy palms or from fermented molasses.

BACARDI: A light-bodied rum. See Rum.

BAILEYS IRISH CREAM: The largest selling liqueur in the world. It is a blend of Irish whiskey, dairy cream and other flavourings. It is a natural product.

BANANA LIQUEUR (LENA): A banana-flavoured liqueur.

BENEDICTINE: A brandy-based liqueur. The perfect end to a perfect meal. Serve straight, with ice, soda, or as part of a favourite cocktail.

BOURBON (WHISKEY): A type of whiskey from the USA with a smooth, easy flavour.

BRANDY: A smooth and mild spirit, mainly produced from the juice of grapes, which is considered a very smooth and palatable drink and ideal for mixing.

BUTTERSCOTCH SCHNAPPS: a butterscotch-flavoured liqueur.

CALVADOS: fine apple brandy made in Normandy.

CAMPARI: A bitter Italian aperitif. Suitable both as a long or short drink, or as a key ingredient in many fashionable cocktails.

CASSIS: A rich purple liqueur that delivers the robust flavour and aroma of blackberries. Cassis lends itself to neat drinking or an endless array of delicious sauces and desserts.

CHAMBORD: A raspberry liqueur.

CHARTREUSE: A liqueur available in yellow or green. Still made by monks of the Carthusian order.

CHERI-SUISSE: A chocolate- and cherry-flavoured liqueur from Switzerland.

CHERRY ADVOCAAT: A morello cherry-flavoured advocaat-based liqueur.

CHERRY BRANDY: Made from concentrated morello cherry juice with a small quantity of bitter almonds and vanilla added. Enjoyable as a neat drink before or after dinner. Excellent for mixers and topping for ice cream.

CHERRY HEERING: A popular dark-red cherry-flavoured liqueur made in Denmark. Known also as Peter Heering.

COCONUT LIQUEUR: A smooth liqueur with the exotic flavour of coconut heightened with light-bodied white rum.

COINTREAU: A liqueur with the aromatic orange flavour of natural citrus fruits. A great mixer and delightful over ice.

CRÈME DE BANANA: Creamy yellow liqueur very similar to banana liqueur.

CRÈME DE CACAO DARK: A rich chocolate liqueur. Smooth and classy. Serve on its own, or mix for all kinds of delectable treats.

CRÈME DE CACAO WHITE: This liqueur delivers a powerful and full-bodied chocolate flavour. An excellent mixer when a chocolate flavour without colour is desired.

CRÈME DE CAFÉ: A sweet brown liqueur made from extracts of coffee.

CRÈME DE CASSIS: A blood-red, sweet, black currant-flavoured liqueur.

CRÈME DE GRAND MARNIER: A very smooth-tasting premium blend of Grand Marnier and French cream, introduced to Australia in 1985. The orange/cognac flavour blends beautifully with the cream.

CRÈME DE MENTHE GREEN: A liqueur with a clear peppermint flavour, reminiscent of a fresh and crisp winter's day in the mountains. An excellent mixer.

CRÈME DE MENTHE WHITE: As for Crème de Menthe Green, when colour is not required.

CURAÇAO BLUE: Slightly bitter liqueur based on natural citrus fruits. Same as Triple Sec but brilliant blue colour is added to make cocktails more exciting.

CURAÇAO ORANGE: Same as Curaçao Blue, but has a strong orange colour and flavour.

CURAÇAO RED: Same as Curaçao Blue, but has a strong red colour.

CURAÇAO TRIPLE SEC: Also known as White Curaçao. As for Blue Curaçao, but without colour. As a liqueur one of the most versatile. Can be enjoyed with or without ice as a neat drink, and is used in more mixed cocktails than any other liqueur.

DRAMBUIE: A Scotch whisky liqueur. Made from a secret recipe dating back to 1745. The names comes from 'An Dram Buidheach', meaning 'the drink that satisfies'.

DUBONNET: A wine-based aperitif from France flavoured with spices and quinine.

FERNET BRANCA: A bitter, aromatic Italian spirit made from over 40 herbs and spices, with a base of grape alcohol. Often served as a digestif.

FRANGELICO: A wild-hazelnut liqueur imported from Italy. Contains infusions of berries and flowers to enrich the flavour.

GALLIANO (LIQUEUR): A classic golden liqueur that blends with a vast array of mixed drinks. Varieties include anise, licorice and vanilla.

GIN: A grain-based spirit whose aroma comes from juniper berries and other rare and subtle herbs. The perfect mixer for both short and long drinks.

GLAYVA: A whisky-based honey and herb-flavoured liqueur from Scotland, similar to Drambuie.

GRAND MARNIER: An orange-flavour liqueur, an original blend of fine old Cognac and extract of oranges. The recipe is over 150 years old.

GRAPPA: An Italian brandy made from distilling grape skins, known as a digestif.

GRENADINE CORDIAL: A grenadine-flavoured non-alcoholic syrup.

IRISH WHISKEY: The distinctive national whiskey of Ireland. Irish Whiskey is distilled three times, not twice. Made from malted barley, unmalted barley, and other grains such as rye and corn.

JÄGERMEISTER: This is a bitter German aperitif flavoured by a complex blend of 56 herbs, fruits and spices.

KAHLÚA: A smooth, dark Mexican liqueur made from real coffee and fine clear spirits.

KIRSCH: A fruit brandy distilled from morello cherries. Delicious drunk straight and excellent in a variety of food recipes.

MALIBU: A clear coconut liqueur based on white rum. Its distinctive taste blends naturally with virtually every mixer available.

MANDARIN NAPOLEON: A Belgian orange liqueur made from cognac flavoured with oils from fresh Sicilian tangerines.

MANGO LIQUEUR (MOHALA): A mango-flavoured liqueur.

MELON LIQUEUR (MIDORI): A soft green liqueur which exudes a refreshing melon flavour. Smooth on the palate. Serve on the rocks, or use to create summertime cocktails.

MINT LIQUEUR: A term for any liqueur with mint flavouring, e.g. crème de menthe, peppermint schnapps, etc.

OPAL NERA: See Sambuca Black.

ORANGE BITTERS: Bitters made from unripe orange rinds infused in alcohol. See also Angostura Bitters.

ORANGE LIQUEUR: An orange-flavoured liqueur.

ORGEAT: A sweet almond-flavoured syrup made also with rose water and orange-flower water.

OUZO: The traditional aperitif of Greece, but now also distilled in Australia. The distinctive flavour of this neutral grain spirit is derived mainly from the seed of the anise plant.

PARFAIT AMOUR: A light-bodied purple French liqueur made from lemons, oranges, brandy and herbs.

PASSIONFRUIT LIQUEUR (PASSOA): A passionfruit-flavoured liqueur.

PEACH LIQUEUR: The delicious flavour of fresh and dried peaches make this a cocktail lover's dream.

PEACHTREE SCHNAPPS: A crystal clear spirit, bursting with the taste of ripe peaches. Drink chilled, on the rocks or mix with any soft drink or juice.

PEAR BRANDY: A digestif made from pears, sometimes sold with a pear in the bottle.

PERNOD: A anise-flavoured French spirit, commonly drunk as an aperitif.

PIMM'S NO. 1 CUP: A gin-based liqueur, flavoured by a secret combination of herbs and spices.

PINEAPPLE LIQUEUR: A sun-filled delight. Delicious neat, a necessity for summertime cocktails.

RUM: A spirit distilled from fermented sugar. Can be dark or light. A light-bodied rum is especially suited for cocktails in which you require subtle aroma and delicate flavour.

RYE WHISKEY (CANADIAN CLUB): Distilled from rye, corn and malted barley. A light, mild and delicate whiskey, ideal for drinking straight or in mixed cocktails.

SABRA: An Israeli liqueur with a unique flavour that comes from tangy jaffa oranges, with a hint of chocolate.

SAMBUCA BLACK: As for clear Sambuca but flavoured with extracts of black elderberry. Opal Nera is a premium Sambuca. Also Galliano Sambuca Black.

SAMBUCA CLEAR: An Italian liqueur made from elderberries with a touch of anise. Also called Galliano Sambuca.

SCOTCH WHISKY: The distinctive national spirit of Scotland. Made from malted barley and other grains.

SOUTHERN COMFORT: A sweet and full-bodied peach-flavoured liqueur based on bourbon whiskey. Its recipe is a secret.

STRAWBERRY LIQUEUR (RUBIS): A fluorescent red liqueur with an unmistakable strawberry bouquet.

STREGA: From Italian origins, Strega is made from orange peel, spices and strong spirits. It is very sweet.

TENNESSEE WHISKEY (JACK DANIEL'S): A type of whiskey distinctive from bourbon, made from the 'old sour mash' process. It is leached through hard maple charcoal, then aged in charred white oak barrels at a controlled temperature, in order to acquire its body, bouquet and colour, while remaining smooth.

TEQUILA: A spirit distilled from the sap of the agave or century plant. A perfect mixer or drink straight with salt and lemon.

TIA MARIA: A rum-based liqueur whose flavour derives from the finest Jamaican coffee. It is not too sweet with a subtle taste of coffee.

TRIPLE SEC: See Curaçao Triple Sec.

VANDERMINT: A rich chocolate liqueur with the added zest of mint.

VERMOUTH: Vermouth is a herbally infused wine, made in France and Italy. Three styles are the most prevalent: Bianco, Rosso and Dry.

VERMOUTH BIANCO: A light, fruity and refreshing Vermouth. Mixes well with soda, lemonade and fruit juices.

VERMOUTH DRY: A crisp, light and dry Vermouth, used as a base for many cocktails.

VERMOUTH ROSSO: This Vermouth has a bitter sweet herbal flavour, and is often drunk as an aperitif.

VODKA: The second highest selling spirit in the world, generally made from grain or potatoes. Most vodkas are filtered through tanks containing charcoal to remove all odours and impurities. Vodka is a premium 40% ABV vodka that is made from the finest grain and 100% filtered water. It is smooth-tasting and remarkably pure.

WHISKY, WHISKEY: See bourbon whiskey, Irish whiskey, rye whiskey, Scotch whisky and Tennessee whiskey.

COCKTAIL RECIPES

A–D

ABC

Ingredients

GLASS

270mL HI-BALL GLASS

MIXERS

5 ICE CUBES

20mL ARMAGNAC

20mL BENEDICTINE

1 dash ANGOSTURA BITTERS

CHAMPAGNE OR SPARKLING WHITE WINE

GARNISH

LEMON SLICE

ORANGE SEGMENTS

MARASCHINO CHERRIES

Method

Crack 2 ice cubes and place them into a shaker with Armagnac, Benedictine and Angostura bitters and shake well. Crush remaining ice cubes and empty into a hi-ball glass. Drain contents of shaker into the crushed ice and top with champagne. Serve garnished with lemon slice, orange segments and cherries.

Acapulco I

Ingredients

GLASS

285mL HI-BALL GLASS

MIXERS

30mL TEQUILA

30mL DARK RUM

30mL TIA MARIA

150mL COCONUT CREAM

ICE CUBES

GARNISH

ORANGE SLICE

Method

Shake ingredients in a shaker. Then strain over ice using a Hawthorn strainer into a 285mL hi-ball glass and serve garnished with an orange slice.

Affinity

Ingredients

GLASS

190mL FANCY CHAMPAGNE GLASS

MIXERS

CRACKED ICE

60mL SCOTCH WHISKY

2 dashes ANGOSTURA BITTERS

30mL DRY VERMOUTH

30mL SWEET VERMOUTH

GARNISH

twist LEMON PEEL

Method

Half fill a mixing glass with cracked ice, add liquid ingredients and stir. Strain into a 190mL champagne glass, garnish with lemon peel and serve.

After Eight

Ingredients

GLASS

50mL FANCY SHOOTER GLASS

MIXERS

15mL KAHLÚA

10mL CRÈME DE MENTHE

20mL BAILEYS IRISH CREAM

GARNISH

twist LEMON PEEL

Method

Layer ingredients in given order into a tall Dutch cordial glass or fancy shooter glass and serve.

Amaretto Sour

Ingredients

GLASS

220mL COCKTAIL GLASS

MIXERS

45mL AMARETTO DI GALLIANO

JUICE OF 1/2 LEMON

SODA WATER

3 ICE CUBES

GARNISH

LIME SLICE

Method

Shake amaretto, lemon juice and ice, pour into a cocktail glass and top with soda. Garnish with a strip of lime peel and serve.

Angel's Kiss

Ingredients

GLASS

290mL POCO GRANDE GLASS

MIXERS

1 scoop VANILLA ICE CREAM

1 tablespoon PASSIONFRUIT PULP

150mL APRICOT NECTAR

CRACKED ICE

GARNISH

MINT LEAVES

Method

Blend all ingredients with ice and pour into glass. Serve garnished with mint leaves.

Comments: A wonderful blend of passionfruit and apricots.

Apple Strawberry Cordial

Ingredients

GLASS

210mL OLD FASHIONED SPIRIT GLASS

MIXERS

1 APPLE, PEELED AND CORED

3 STRAWBERRIES, LEAVES REMOVED

30mL SCOTCH WHISKY

1 teaspoon BROWN SUGAR

1 PINCH ALLSPICE, NUTMEG

CRACKED ICE

GARNISH

1 STRAWBERRY

GROUND NUTMEG

Method

Blend over ice and pour into glass. Garnish with a strawberry and sprinkle of nutmeg.

April Shower

Ingredients

GLASS

300mL HI-BALL GLASS

MIXERS

30mL BRANDY

60mL ORANGE JUICE

30mL BENEDICTINE

2 ICE CUBES

SODA WATER (TO TOP UP)

GARNISH

2 CHERRIES

Method

Pour all ingredients except soda into glass. Stir, top up with soda water and garnish with cherries. Serve with straws.

Aquavit Fizz

Ingredients

GLASS

170mL TULIP CHAMPAGNE FLUTE

MIXERS

45mL AQUAVIT

30mL LEMON JUICE

15mL CHERRY HEERING

10mL SUGAR SYRUP

1 EGG WHITE

SODA WATER

ICE CUBES

Method

Shake all ingredients with ice and strain into glass. Then top up with soda water.

Astronaut

Ingredients

GLASS

285mL HI-BALL GLASS

MIXERS

30mL DARK RUM

30mL VODKA

10mL FRESH LEMON JUICE

6 drops PASSIONFRUIT PULP

ICE CUBES

GARNISH

½ scoop PASSIONFRUIT

Method

Shake all ingredients over ice and strain into glass. Garnish with ½ scoop of passionfruit.

Avalanche

Ingredients

GLASS

190mL FLUTED WINE GLASS

MIXERS

30mL COINTREAU

30mL ORANGE JUICE

30mL TIA MARIA

50mL CREAM

ICE CUBES

Method

Shake all ingredients with ice. Then strain into glass to serve.

B&B

Ingredients

GLASS

BRANDY BALLOON GLASS

MIXERS

30mL COGNAC

30mL BENEDICTINE

Method

Build, no ice.

Comments: Tempt your pallet with this delicious combination of fine liqueurs. Relaxing by the fire on winter nights, the connoisseur will enjoy interesting conversation with friends over this drink. Ideal with coffee.

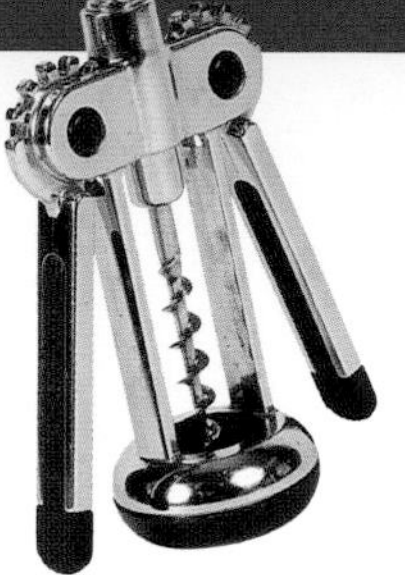

B52

Ingredients

GLASS

185mL OLD FASHIONED SPIRIT GLASS

MIXERS

30mL KAHLÚA

30mL BAILEYS IRISH CREAM

30mL GRAND MARNIER

CRUSHED ICE

Method

Place a scoop full of crushed ice into glass. Layer ingredients and serve.

Bacardi Blossom

Ingredients

GLASS

90mL FANCY MARTINI GLASS

MIXERS

40mL BACARDI RUM

3 ICE CUBES

10mL ORANGE JUICE

10mL LEMON JUICE

1 teaspoon SUGAR

GARNISH

twist LEMON RIND

Method

Shake all ingredients and strain into glass. Serve garnished with lemon rind.

Bad Girl

Ingredients

GLASS

145mL CHAMPAGNE SAUCER

MIXERS

15mL MALIBU

10mL GALLIANO LIQUEUR

15mL BANANA LIQUEUR

30mL CREAM

15mL ADVOCAAT

CRACKED ICE

GARNISH

1 STRAWBERRY

Method

Blend ingredients with ice, pour into glass and serve garnished with strawberry.

Badminton

Ingredients

GLASS

250mL RED WINE GLASS

MIXERS

120mL RED WINE

1 teaspoon SUGAR

1 pinch NUTMEG

SODA WATER

GARNISH

CUCUMBER SLICE, CUT LENGTHWAYS

Method

Stir sugar into red wine and add nutmeg, then top up with soda water. Serve garnished with cucumber slice.

Baltimore Zoo

Ingredients

GLASS

300mL FOOTED PILSENER GLASS

MIXERS

15mL DARK RUM

15mL GIN

15mL COINTREAU

60mL CRANBERRY JUICE

BEER

ICE CUBES

Method

Shake all ingredients with ice and strain into glass. Then top up with beer.

Banana Colada

Ingredients

GLASS

300mL FANCY GLASS

MIXERS

30mL BACARDI RUM

30mL SUGAR SYRUP

30mL COCONUT CREAM

30mL CREAM

120mL PINEAPPLE JUICE

1/2 BANANA

CRACKED ICE

GARNISH

BANANA SLICE

PINEAPPLE WEDGE AND LEAVES

SPEARMINT AND MINT LEAVES

Method

Blend with ice and pour into glass. Garnish with a slice of banana, pineapple wedge and leaves, spearmint and mint leaves. Serves with straws.

Comments: An exemplary cocktail to demonstrate the variety of fruits available, particularly in Australia. You can modify this cocktail with your own selection of exotic fruit.

Banshee

Ingredients

GLASS

BRANDY BALLOON

MIXERS

30mL DARK RUM

60mL CREAM

20mL CRÈME DE CACAO

1 BANANA

15mL BANANA LIQUEUR

GARNISH

3 CHERRIES

Method

Blend all ingredients until smooth and pour into glass. Serve garnished with cherries.

Bellini (Frozen)

Ingredients

GLASS

140mL CHAMPAGNE FLUTE

MIXERS

60mL PEACH SLICES WITH SYRUP

30mL VODKA

30mL PEACH LIQUEUR

1 teaspoon SUGAR

CHAMPAGNE

CRACKED ICE

Method

Blend with ice, then strain into glass. Top up with champagne.

Belly Dancer

Ingredients

GLASS

90mL COCKTAIL GLASS

MIXERS

30mL CREAM

15mL LIME JUICE

60mL COCONUT CREAM

15mL GRENADINE CORDIAL

ICE CUBES

GARNISH

GRATED COCONUT

Method

Shake all ingredients over ice and strain into glass. Garnish with grated coconut.

Bermuda Triangle

Ingredients

GLASS

140mL
COCKTAIL GLASS

MIXERS

30mL BLUE CURAÇAO

60mL PINEAPPLE JUICE

30mL BACARDI RUM

CRUSHED ICE

20mL AMARETTO DI GALLIANO

GARNISH

PINEAPPLE WEDGE

Method

Blend all ingredients until smooth, then pour into glass. Garnish with pineapple wedge to serve.

Betsy Ross

Ingredients

GLASS

BRANDY BALLOON

MIXERS

30mL BRANDY

30mL PORT WINE

5mL COINTREAU

4–5 dashes OF ANGOSTURA BITTERS

ICE CUBES

Method

Shake all ingredients over ice and strain into glass.

Between the Sheets

Ingredients

GLASS

140mL CHAMPAGNE SAUCER

MIXERS

30mL BRANDY

30mL BACARDI RUM

30mL COINTREAU

15mL LEMON JUICE

ICE CUBES

GARNISH

twist LEMON RIND

Method

Shake all ingredients with ice and strain into glass. Garnish with twist of lemon rind.

Comments: A pre-dinner cocktail. A fine blend of traditional spirits for the mature palate.

Black Velvet

Ingredients

GLASS

140mL CHAMPAGNE SAUCER

MIXERS

70mL CHAMPAGNE

70mL STOUT

Method

Build in glass and stir.

Blackjack

Ingredients

GLASS

130mL COCKTAIL GLASS

MIXERS

30mL KIRSCH

45mL FRESH COFFEE

10mL BRANDY

CRUSHED ICE

GARNISH

COFFEE GRANULES

Method

Stir all ingredients with ice in a mixing glass and pour into cocktail glass. Serve garnished with coffee granules.

Blood & Sand

Ingredients

GLASS

145mL CHAMPAGNE SAUCER

MIXERS

30mL SCOTCH WHISKY

30mL ORANGE JUICE

30mL CHERRY BRANDY

CRACKED ICE

30mL SWEET VERMOUTH (ROSSO OR BIANCO)

GARNISH

1 twist ORANGE RIND

Method

Half fill mixing glass with cracked ice, add other ingredients and stir. Strain into champagne saucer and garnish with orange rind to serve.

Bloodhound

Ingredients

GLASS

145mL COCKTAIL GLASS

MIXERS

15mL DRY VERMOUTH

3 dashes STRAWBERRY LIQUEUR

15mL GIN

2 STRAWBERRIES, LEAVES REMOVED

15mL SWEET VERMOUTH (ROSSO OR BIANCO)

4 ICE CUBES

GARNISH

2 STRAWBERRIES

Method

Blend two ice cubes, gin, both types of vermouth, strawberry liqueur and two strawberries. Pour into glass over remaining ice cubes. Garnish with remaining strawberries to serve.

Bloody Mary

Ingredients

GLASS

285mL HI-BALL GLASS

MIXERS

60mL VODKA
1 dash WORCESTERSHIRE SAUCE
10mL LEMON JUICE
2–3 drops TABASCO SAUCE
TOMATO JUICE
3 ICE CUBES
SALT
PEPPER

Method

Into glass pour vodka, sauces, lemon juices and a sprinkle of salt and pepper. Top up with tomato juice and ice cubes and serve with swizzle stick and straws.

Note: White rum or tequila may be used instead of vodka.

Blue French

Ingredients

GLASS

285mL HI-BALL GLASS

MIXERS

30mL PERNOD

5mL LEMON JUICE

5mL BLUE CURAÇAO

BITTER LEMON (SOFT DRINK)

ICE CUBES

GARNISH

LEMON WHEEL

Method

Build over ice in glass. Top up with bitter lemon. Garnish with lemon wheel, and serve with straws.

Blue Lagoon

Ingredients

GLASS

BRANDY BALLOON

MIXERS

30mL GIN

10mL BLUE CURAÇAO

LEMONADE

GARNISH

LEMON WHEEL

Method

Build gin and curaçao over ice and top up with lemonade. Garnish with lemon wheel.

Comments: Named after the movie which bears this cocktails name.

Bolshoi Punch

Ingredients

GLASS

285mL FOOTED
HI-BALL GLASS

MIXERS

30mL VODKA

10mL DARK RUM

10mL CRÈME DE CASSIS

15mL LIME JUICE

15mL LEMON JUICE

BITTER LEMON (SOFT DRINK)

ICE CUBES

GARNISH

1 ORANGE SLICE

1 RED CHERRY

Method

Blend all ingredients with ice and strain into glass, then top up with bitter lemon. Garnish with orange slice and red cherry.

Bosom Caresser

Ingredients

GLASS

140mL CHAMPAGNE SAUCER

MIXERS

30mL BRANDY

15mL ORANGE LIQUEUR

5mL GRENADINE CORDIAL

1 EGG YOLK

ICE CUBES

GARNISH

2 CHERRIES

Method

Shake all ingredients with ice and strain into glass. Garnish with two red cherries, slit on side of glass.

Comments: Close to every lady's heart! Egg yolk allows the cocktail to breathe, supporting the brandy's body and bounce. Fine on any occasion.

Boston Cream

Ingredients

GLASS

130mL COCKTAIL GLASS

MIXERS

30mL CREAM

15mL LIME JUICE

30mL COCONUT CREAM

15mL GRENADINE CORDIAL

ICE CUBES

GARNISH

CHOCOLATE SPRINKLES

Method

Shake all ingredients over ice and strain into glass. Garnish with a cross made of chocolate sprinkles.

Bourbon Banana

Ingredients

GLASS

BRANDY BALLOON

MIXERS

30mL BOURBON

30mL ORANGE JUICE

30mL KAHLÚA

30mL CREAM

1 BANANA

CRUSHED ICE

Method

Blend ingredients with ice and serve in a brandy balloon.

Brandy Alexander

Ingredients

GLASS

140mL CHAMPAGNE SAUCER

MIXERS

30mL BRANDY

30mL DARK CRÈME DE CACAO

5mL GRENADINE CORDIAL

30mL CREAM

ICE CUBES

GARNISH

GROUND NUTMEG

1 CHERRY

Method

Shake with ice and strain. Sprinkle nutmeg over a pair of crossed plastic straws to make a cross pattern. Garnish with a cherry.

Comments: An after-dinner cocktail. An Alexander uses Green Crème de Menthe instead of Crème de Cacao. Cognac may be substituted for Brandy to deliver an exceptional aftertaste.

Brandy Crusta

Ingredients

GLASS

CHAMPAGNE SAUCER, SUGAR-FROSTED

MIXERS

90mL BRANDY

1 dash ANGOSTURA BITTERS

3 dashes MARASCHINO

GARNISH

1 MARASCHINO CHERRY

Method

Frost rim of glass with sugar before starting. Shake all ingredients and strain into glass, being careful not to remove sugar. Garnish with cherry.

Brandy, Lime & Soda

Ingredients

GLASS

285mL FOOTED HI-BALL GLASS

MIXERS

45mL BRANDY

CRACKED ICE

15mL LIME JUICE

SODA WATER

GARNISH

1 LIME OR LEMON WHEEL

Method

Pour brandy and lime juice over one scoop of ice into glass. Top up with soda water, garnish with lime or lemon wheel and serve with straws.

Brazilian Monk

Ingredients

GLASS

285mL TULIP WINE GLASS

MIXERS

30mL KAHLÚA

15mL FRANGELICO

15mL DARK CRÈME DE CACAO

2 scoops VANILLA ICE CREAM

CRUSHED ICE

Method

Blend all ingredients with ice and pour into glass. Garnish with a wild flower or flower petals.

Comments: Frangelico is imported from Italy and made from wild flowers infused into hazelnuts.

Brittany

Ingredients

GLASS

150mL OLD FASHIONED SPIRIT GLASS

MIXERS

30mL GIN

15mL AMER PICON

10mL ORANGE JUICE

10mL LEMON JUICE

CRUSHED ICE

Method

Blend all ingredients with ice and pour into glass.

Bronx

Ingredients

GLASS

90mL FANCY COCKTAIL GLASS

MIXERS

30mL GIN

15mL ORANGE JUICE

1 dash FRENCH VERMOUTH (WHITE)

CRACKED ICE

1 dash ITALIAN VERMOUTH (BIANCO)

GARNISH

ORANGE SLICE

Method

Shake and strain into glass. Serve garnished with orange slice.

Cabaret

Ingredients

GLASS

130mL COCKTAIL GLASS

MIXERS

30mL GIN

30mL DUBONNET

5mL PERNOD

5 dashes ANGOSTURA BITTERS

ICE CUBES

GARNISH

RED CHERRY

Method

Stir in mixing glass over ice and strain into cocktail glass. Garnish with cherry.

Café De Paris

Ingredients

GLASS

130mL COCKTAIL GLASS

MIXERS

60mL GIN

10mL DOUBLE CREAM

5mL PERNOD

1 EGG WHITE

ICE CUBES

GARNISH

LEMON SLICE

Method

Shake all ingredients over ice and strain into glass. Garnish with slice of lemon.

Café Oscar

Ingredients

GLASS

250mL IRISH COFFEE MUG

MIXERS

20mL KAHLÚA

20mL AMARETTO DI GALLIANO

HOT COFFEE

DOUBLE CREAM

GARNISH

1 scoop VANILLA ICE CREAM

Method

Pour spirits into glass, then top up with coffee. Float cream on top. Garnish with ice cream.

Caper's Caper

Ingredients

GLASS

285mL HI-BALL GLASS

MIXERS

30mL ADVOCAAT

1/4 AVOCADO

30mL FRANGELICO

1 scoop ICE CREAM

4–5 STRAWBERRIES

CRUSHED ICE

GARNISH

COFFEE BEAN

1 STRAWBERRY

Method

Blend ingredients with ice and pour into glass. Garnish with coffee bean and strawberry and serve with straws.

Cardamom Spice

Ingredients

GLASS

270mL FOOTED HI-BALL GLASS

MIXERS

BROWN SUGAR LUMP

CARDAMOM ESSENCE

CRACKED ICE

60mL SCOTCH WHISKY

Method

Infuse brown sugar lump with three drops cardamom essence. Add ice, then pour over whiskey. Stir.

Comments: The warm, sweet spicy flavour of cardamom combines with scotch whisky to create a sensational drink. You can also serve without the ice for a delicious winter cocktail.

Caribbean Champagne

Ingredients

GLASS

140mL CHAMPAGNE SAUCER

MIXERS

100mL CHAMPAGNE

10mL BACARDI RUM

10mL BANANA LIQUEUR

5mL ORANGE BITTERS

GARNISH

BANANA SLICE

Method

Stir all ingredients without ice and pour into glass. Garnish with slice of banana.

Chablis Cup

Ingredients

GLASS

285mL FOOTED HI-BALL GLASS

MIXERS

20mL GRAND MARNIER

15mL KIRSCH

1 PEACH SLICE

1 BANANA SLICE

1 ORANGE SLICE, NO RIND

1 LEMON SLICE, NO RIND

1 MINT SPRIG

60mL CHABLIS (WINE)

GARNISH

ASSORTED FRUIT SLICES

Method

Blend all ingredients over ice, pour into glass, then top up with Chablis. Serve garnished with fruit.

Chambord Margarita

Ingredients

GLASS

350mL MARGARITA GLASS, SALT-FROSTED

MIXERS

45mL TEQUILA

15mL CHAMBORD RASPBERRY LIQUEUR

90mL SOUR MIX

CRUSHED ICE

Method

Blend the ingredients with ice and serve.

Note: To make sour mix, see page 7.

Champagne Cocktail

Ingredients

GLASS

140mL CHAMPAGNE FLUTE

MIXERS

1 SUGAR CUBE

6 drops ANGOSTURA BITTERS

15mL COGNAC OR BRANDY

CHAMPAGNE OR SPARKLING WHITE WINE

GARNISH

RED CHERRY

Method

Soak sugar cube in Angostura Bitters in flute, before adding brandy. Then top with Champagne. Garnish with red cherry (optional).

Champagne St Moritz

Ingredients

GLASS

140mL CHAMPAGNE SAUCER

MIXERS

10mL GIN

10mL APRICOT BRANDY

10mL ORANGE JUICE

CHAMPAGNE OR SPARKLING WHITE WINE

ICE CUBES

GARNISH

ORANGE SLICE

Method

Shake over ice and strain, then top up with Champagne. Garnish with orange slice.

Cherries Jubilee

Ingredients

GLASS

140mL COCKTAIL GLASS

MIXERS

30mL CHERRY ADVOCAAT

30mL WHITE CRÈME DE CACAO

15mL MALIBU

40mL CREAM

15mL MILK

ICE CUBES

GARNISH

GRATED CHOCOLATE

1 CHERRY

COCONUT RIND

Method

Shake with ice and strain into glass. Garnish with grated chocolate and cherry and coconut rind on side of glass.

Comments: Created by Leah Johns, this cocktail won first place in Seagram's National Liqueur Championships, Hobart, Tasmania, 1990.

Cherry Bomb

Ingredients

GLASS

270mL MARGARITA GLASS, SUGAR-FROSTED

MIXERS

1 teaspoon CASTER SUGAR
5mL GRENADINE CORDIAL
30mL VODKA
15mL CHERRY BRANDY
LEMONADE
CRUSHED ICE

GARNISH

ORCHID (OPTIONAL)

Method

Colour sugar with grenadine and prepare glass by sugar-frosting the rim.

Blend other ingredients over ice and pour into glass, then top up with lemonade. Garnish with an orchid.

Comments: Watch as the magical colour fizzes up like a Cherry Bomb.

Chi Chi

Ingredients

GLASS

CHAMPAGNE SAUCER

MIXERS

45mL VODKA
20mL COCONUT CREAM
20mL MALIBU
15mL LIME CORDIAL
15mL LEMON CORDIAL
1 slice PINEAPPLE
60mL PINEAPPLE JUICE
1 dash CREAM
ICE CUBES

GARNISH

PINEAPPLE WEDGE

Method

Blend ingredients with ice until smooth. Pour into a champagne saucer and serve garnished with pineapple wedge.

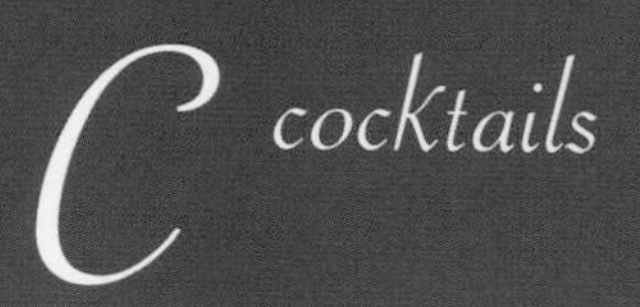

Chicago

Ingredients

GLASS

140mL COCKTAIL GLASS

MIXERS

40mL BRANDY

1 dash ANGOSTURA BITTERS

5mL COINTREAU

2 ICE CUBES

SPARKLING WHITE WINE

Method

Pour spirits into glass over ice, top up with white wine and serve.

Chiquita

Ingredients

GLASS

250mL WINE GLASS

MIXERS

45mL VODKA

10mL BANANA LIQUEUR

10mL LIME JUICE

1/2 BANANA, SLICED

pinch SUGAR

ICE CUBES

GARNISH

BANANA SLICE

Method

Blend all ingredients with ice and pour into glass. Garnish with banana slice.

Chocolate-Covered Cherry

Ingredients

GLASS

250mL IRISH COFFEE MUG, PREHEATED

MIXERS

30mL CHERRY LIQUEUR

HOT CHOCOLATE

GARNISH

WHIPPING CREAM FROM AEROSOL CAN

1 RED CHERRY

Method

Pour in liqueur, then top up with hot chocolate. Garnish with whipping cream and red cherry.

Cliff Hanger

Ingredients

GLASS

145mL COCKTAIL GLASS

MIXERS

40mL VODKA

15mL CHERRY HEERING

LEMONADE

15mL GALLIANO LIQUEUR

Method

Place 2 ice cubes into glass, then pour vodka and Cherry Heering over top. Top up with lemonade, float Galliano Liqueur and serve.

Clover Blossom

Ingredients

GLASS

270mL HI-BALL GLASS

MIXERS

60mL LEMON CORDIAL

30mL LIME JUICE

1 EGG WHITE

1 dash GRENADINE CORDIAL

TONIC WATER

ICE CUBES

GARNISH

SLICE OF LEMON

MINT LEAF

Method

Blend all ingredients with ice and pour into glass. Garnish with slice of lemon, mint leaf and a straw.

Comments: A delicate fluffy concoction.

Cointreau Caipirinha

Ingredients

GLASS

175mL PRISM ROCKS GLASS

MIXERS

30mL COINTREAU

¼ FRESH LIME OR LEMON

CRUSHED ICE

Method

Cut lime into pieces and place in glass. Extract juice by using a pestle (muddling). Fill glass with crushed ice and add Cointreau. Stir.

Cointreauversial

Ingredients

GLASS

285mL HI-BALL GLASS

MIXERS

10mL MANGO PURÉE

2–3 STRAWBERRIES

2–3 KIWIFRUIT CHUNKS

2–3 FRESH MINT LEAVES

20mL COINTREAU

45mL VODKA

10mL STRAWBERRY LIQUEUR

LEMONADE OR SODA WATER

ICE CUBES

GARNISH

LIME WHEEL

MINT LEAF

Method

Muddle fruit and mint in a glass, build alcohol over ice, stir well. Top up with lemonade or soda water.

Columbia Skin

Ingredients

GLASS

300mL BEER MUG

MIXERS

½ LEMON, THINLY PEELED

30mL SCOTCH WHISKY

1 cup (250mL) BOILING WATER

GARNISH

LEMON SLICE

Method

Pour Scotch and boiling water over lemon half. Garnish with a slice of lemon.

Commonwealth

Ingredients

GLASS

150mL OLD FASHIONED SPIRIT GLASS

MIXERS

30mL CANADIAN CLUB RYE WHISKY

15mL VANDERMINT LIQUEUR

15mL LEMON JUICE

GARNISH

LEMON SLICE

Method

Shake all ingredients over ice and strain into glass. Garnish with a slice of lemon.

Copacabana

Ingredients

GLASS

90mL COCKTAIL GLASS

MIXERS

25mL APRICOT BRANDY

15mL LEMON JUICE

15mL BRANDY

15mL COINTREAU

CRUSHED ICE

GARNISH

ORANGE WHEEL

Method

Shake all ingredients and strain into a glass. Garnish with orange wheel.

Copenhagen Special

Ingredients

GLASS

150mL CHAMPAGNE FLUTE

MIXERS

30mL AQUAVIT

30mL ARRACK

15mL LEMON JUICE

ICE CUBES

GARNISH

LEMON SLICE

Method

Shake all ingredients over ice and strain into glass. Garnish with a slice of lemon.

Crimson Tide

Ingredients

GLASS

OLD FASHIONED SPIRIT GLASS

MIXERS

6–8 FRESH RASPBERRIES

1/2 teaspoon SUGAR

CRUSHED ICE

10mL LIME JUICE

30mL FRANGELICO

30mL ABSOLUT KURANT

1 dash CHAMBORD RASPBERRY LIQUEUR

GARNISH

FRESH RASPBERRIES

MINT SPRIG

Method

Muddle the raspberries and sugar in a shaker. Add ice and remaining ingredients. Shake and pour into an old fashioned glass. Garnish with fresh raspberries and a mint sprig.

Crush Bus

Ingredients

GLASS

210mL OLD FASHIONED SPIRIT GLASS

MIXERS

4–5 STRAWBERRIES

MINT LEAVES

15mL SUGAR SYRUP

30mL FRANGELICO

15mL RUBIS STRAWBERRY LIQUEUR

15mL TIA MARIA

CRACKED ICE

Method

Muddle the strawberries, mint and sugar in glass. Add the remaining ingredients. Stir vigorously and serve.

Czar's Delight

Ingredients

GLASS

290mL OLD FASHIONED SPIRIT GLASS

MIXERS

30mL VODKA

75mL CREAM

30mL PEPPERMINT LIQUEUR

150mL MILK

2 ICE CUBES

GARNISH

MINT LEAVES, FROSTED WITH SUGAR

Method

Shake ingredients and pour into glass, garnish with mint leaves and serve.

Daiquiri (assorted)

Ingredients

GLASS

270mL FOOTED HI-BALL GLASS

MIXERS

30mL LIQUEUR TO MATCH FRUIT (MIDORI, RUBIS, LENA OR MOHALA)

30mL BACARDI RUM

45mL LEMON JUICE

15mL LIME CORDIAL OR SUGAR SYRUP

3–4 pieces OF APPROPRIATE FRUIT (HONEYDEW MELON, STRAWBERRY, BANANA OR MANGO)

CRUSHED ICE

GARNISH

FRUIT SLICES

Method

Choose liqueur to match desired fruit. Blend ingredients with ice. Garnished with appropriate fruit slices.

Daiquiri Original

Ingredients

GLASS

200mL FANCY COCKTAIL GLASS, CHILLED

MIXERS

90mL WHITE RUM

1 teaspoon SUGAR

30mL LEMON OR LIME JUICE

ICE CUBES

GARNISH

LEMON SLICE

Method

Shake all ingredients with ice and strain into chilled cocktail glass. Garnish with lemon slice and serve.

Daiquiri Strawberry

Ingredients

GLASS

300mL COCKTAIL GLASS

MIXERS

90mL WHITE RUM

30mL LEMON JUICE

5 mL STRAWBERRY LIQUEUR

60mL MILK

10 STRAWBERRIES

CRUSHED ICE

GARNISH

1 STRAWBERRY

Method

Blend all ingredients until smooth, pour into glass, garnish with a strawberry and serve.

Death by Chocolate

Ingredients

GLASS

CHAMPAGNE SAUCER

MIXERS

30mL BAILEYS IRISH CREAM

30mL CRÈME DE CACAO

30mL KAHLÚA

90mL THICKENED CREAM

30mL TIA MARIA

ICE CUBES

GARNISH

GRATED CHOCOLATE

Method

Shake with ice and strain into a champagne saucer. Garnish with grated chocolate and serve.

Desert Rose

Ingredients

GLASS

270mL FOOTED HI-BALL GLASS

MIXERS

30mL MIDORI MELON LIQUEUR

60mL PINEAPPLE JUICE

30mL BAILEYS IRISH CREAM

60g ROCKMELON

15mL GLAYVA

CRUSHED ICE

GARNISH

PINEAPPLE WEDGE

Method

Blend all ingredients with ice and pour into glass. Garnish with pineapple wedge and serve with straws.

Desert Storm

Ingredients

GLASS

140mL FANCY COCKTAIL GLASS

MIXERS

15mL MANGO LIQUEUR

60mL PINEAPPLE JUICE

15mL BACARDI RUM

1 dash TABASCO SAUCE

15mL GIN

ICE CUBES

GARNISH

2 CHERRY TOMATOES

Method

Shake with ice. Strain into glass. Serve garnished with cherry tomatoes.

Diplomat

Ingredients

GLASS

225mL FOOTED HI-BALL GLASS

MIXERS

45mL VODKA

90mL PINEAPPLE JUICE

45mL MIDORI MELON LIQUEUR

5mL LEMON JUICE

ICE CUBES

GARNISH

LIME WHEEL

Method

Shake all ingredients with ice. Strain into glass and serve with straws.

Dizzy Blond

Ingredients

GLASS

285mL HI-BALL GLASS

MIXERS

60mL ADVOCAAT

LEMONADE

30mL PERNOD

CRACKED ICE

GARNISH

1 MARASCHINO CHERRY

Method

Half fill glass with cracked ice and add advocaat and Pernod. Top up with lemonade, garnish with cherry and serve.

Dizzy Whistle

Ingredients

GLASS

90mL MARTINI GLASS

MIXERS

15mL FRANGELICO

10mL PINEAPPLE JUICE

10mL GREEN CRÈME DE MENTHE

10mL CREAM

Method

Layer pineapple juice onto Frangelico. Then shake Green Crème de Menthe with cream in shaker and layer onto cocktail.

Dolomint

Ingredients

GLASS

225mL FANCY HI-BALL GLASS

MIXERS

30mL GIN

30mL GALLIANO LIQUEUR

30mL LIME JUICE

SODA WATER

FRESH MINT LEAVES

GARNISH

MINT SPRIG

Method

Pour alcohol and lime juice into glass over ice and top up with soda water. Decorate rim of glass with sprig of mint and add 2 fresh mint leaves.

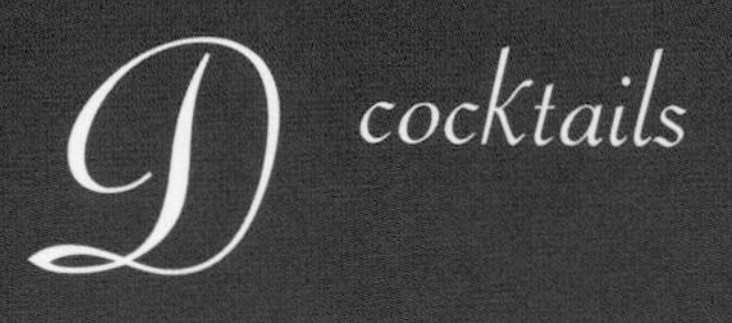

Drambuie High

Ingredients

GLASS

285mL FOOTED HI-BALL GLASS

MIXERS

30mL DRAMBUIE

20mL COCONUT CREAM

30mL GOLDEN RUM

30mL PINEAPPLE JUICE

30mL CREAM

$^{1}/_{2}$ BANANA

1 scoop CRUSHED ICE

GARNISH

PINEAPPLE LEAVES

Method

Blend all ingredients until smooth, pour into glass. Garnish with pineapple leaves and serve.

Dubonnet Fizz

Ingredients

GLASS

285mL HI-BALL GLASS, CHILLED

MIXERS

30mL DUBONNET

30mL CHERRY LIQUEUR

30mL ORANGE JUICE

15mL LEMON JUICE

SODA WATER

ICE CUBES

GARNISH

twist LEMON RIND

1 RED CHERRY

Method

Shake all ingredients over ice and pour into glass. Then top up with soda water. Garnish with lemon rind and red cherry.

Dyevtchka

Ingredients

GLASS

300mL FANCY COCKTAIL GLASS

MIXERS

30mL VODKA

30mL COINTREAU

20mL FRESH LIME JUICE

20mL FRESH LEMON JUICE

15mL PINEAPPLE JUICE

ICE CUBES

GARNISH

PINEAPPLE WEDGE

CHERRIES

Method

Shake all ingredients with ice and pour into glass. Garnish with pineapple wedge and cherry.

Comments: This drink will open up the hidden secrets of the formerly communist eastern bloc of Europe.

COCKTAIL RECIPES

E–H

Early Summer

Ingredients

GLASS

115mL COCKTAIL GLASS

MIXERS

30mL GIN

30mL ORANGE JUICE

30mL APRICOT BRANDY

30mL CALVADOS

CRACKED ICE

GARNISH

1 slice APPLE

Method

Shake all ingredients with ice and strain into glass. Garnish with apple slice and serve.

East Wind

Ingredients

GLASS

90mL FANCY MARTINI GLASS

MIXERS

30mL VODKA

2–3 dashes WHITE RUM

15mL DRY VERMOUTH

15mL WHITE VERMOUTH

CRACKED ICE

GARNISH

LIME SLICE

Method

Shake all ingredients with ice and strain into glass to serve.

Eldorado

Ingredients

GLASS

115mL COCKTAIL GLASS

MIXERS

30mL WHITE RUM

30mL ADVOCAAT

30mL CRÈME DE CACAO

GARNISH

1 teaspoon GRATED COCONUT

Method

Shake all ingredients with ice. Strain into glass. Garnish with grated coconut to serve.

Electric Blue

Ingredients

GLASS

270mL FOOTED HI-BALL GLASS

MIXERS

15mL VODKA

30mL DRY VERMOUTH

15mL BLUE CURAÇAO

LEMONADE

GARNISH

LIME SLICE

Method

Pour vodka, vermouth and curaçao over ice into glass. Top up with lemonade and serve, garnished with lime slice.

Elephant Walk

Ingredients

GLASS

210mL OLD FASHIONED SPIRIT GLASS

MIXERS

30mL GIN

1 dash ANGOSTURA BITTERS

15mL TEQUILA

1 dash GRENADINE CORDIAL

15mL ORANGE JUICE

CRACKED ICE

GARNISH

1/2 ORANGE SLICE

LEMON SLICE

1 stick CUCUMBER

Method

Fill glass with cracked ice, build ingredients, and garnish with fruit and cucumber. Add swizzle stick and serve.

Emerald Queen

Ingredients

GLASS

145mL CHAMPAGNE SAUCER

MIXERS

60mL VODKA

10mL BLUE CURAÇAO

40mL DRY VERMOUTH

20mL GALLIANO LIQUEUR

CRACKED ICE

GARNISH

1 MARASCHINO CHERRY

Method

Half fill mixing glass with cracked ice, add ingredients and stir. Strain into glass, garnish with cherry and serve.

Eton Blazer

Ingredients

GLASS

285mL FOOTED HI-BALL GLASS

MIXERS

25mL GIN

15mL LEMON JUICE

25mL KIRSCH

SODA WATER

2 teaspoon SUGAR SYRUP

CRACKED ICE

GARNISH

3 MARASCHINO CHERRIES

Method

Place all ingredients except soda water and cherries into glass. Top up with soda water, garnish with cherries and serve.

Fallen Angel

Ingredients

GLASS

285mL HI-BALL GLASS

MIXERS

20mL ADVOCAAT

20mL CHERRY BRANDY

LEMONADE

GARNISH

RED CHERRY OR STRAWBERRY

Method

Build alcohol over ice and stir. Top up with lemonade. Garnish with red cherry or strawberry. Serve with straws.

Comments: Ensure advocaat and cherry brandy is mixed thoroughly before topping up with lemonade. The unstirred version of this cocktail is known as a Ruptured Rooster.

Flirt with Dirt

Ingredients

GLASS

90mL COCKTAIL GLASS

MIXERS

30mL KAHLÚA

30mL MALIBU

15mL VANDERMINT

15mL FRESH CREAM

ICE CUBES

GARNISH

1 MARASCHINO CHERRY

Method

Shake Kahlúa, Vandermint and Malibu with ice and strain into glass. Float cream and serve.

Fluffy Duck No. 1

Ingredients

GLASS

285mL HI-BALL GLASS

MIXERS

30mL BACARDI RUM

30mL ADVOCAAT

LEMONADE

30mL FRESH CREAM

GARNISH

LEMON WHEEL

Method

Build alcohol over ice. Top up with lemonade. Float cream. Garnish with a lemon wheel. Serve with straws.

Comments: Many cocktail bars shake ingredients with cream before topping up with lemonade.

Fluffy Duck No. 2

Ingredients

GLASS

140mL CHAMPAGNE SAUCER

MIXERS

30mL BACARDI RUM

30mL ADVOCAAT

30mL ORANGE JUICE

30mL CREAM

ICE CUBES

GARNISH

1 ORANGE SLICE

1 RED CHERRY

Method

Shake all ingredients with ice and strain into glass. Garnish with orange slice and red cherry.

Comments: An after-dinner variation of the popular fluffy duck cocktail. A smoother and shorter drink.

Flying Dutchman

Ingredients

GLASS

185mL OLD FASHIONED SPIRIT GLASS

MIXERS

10mL COINTREAU

30mL GIN

ICE CUBES

GARNISH

twist LEMON RIND

Method

Coat glass with Cointreau then pour gin into glass over ice. Garnish with lemon twist.

Fourth of July

Ingredients

GLASS

140mL CHAMPAGNE SAUCER

MIXERS

22mL BOURBON

22mL KAHLÚA

22mL GALLIANO LIQUEUR

22mL ORANGE JUICE

22mL FRESH CREAM

GARNISH

STRAWBERRY

pinch CINNAMON

Method

Shake all ingredients with ice and strain into glass. Serve sprinkled with cinnamon and garnished with strawberry.

Comments: Warm the champagne saucer with hot water, swirl the Galliano around and add the Bourbon. Shake the Kahlúa, orange juice and cream over ice. Ignite the Galliano and Bourbon and sprinkle cinnamon onto the flames to achieve a fireworks effect. Strain the shaken ingredients into glass to extinguish the flames.

A variation of this drink is the 'Flaming Love' in which the Bourbon is omitted, making the drink less alcoholic and smoother.

Frangelico Caipiroska

Ingredients

GLASS

OLD FASHIONED SPIRIT GLASS

MIXERS

8 LIME CHUNKS

1 teaspoon RAW SUGAR

30mL FRANGELICO

30mL VODKA

60mL CRANBERRY JUICE

ICE CUBES

Method

Muddle lime and sugar in glass. Add alcohol, ice and top with cranberry juice. Stir vigorously and serve.

Frangelico Luau

Ingredients

GLASS

285mL HI-BALL GLASS

MIXERS

45mL FRANGELICO

200mL PINEAPPLE JUICE

1 dash GRENADINE CORDIAL

CRACKED ICE

GARNISH

1 PINEAPPLE SLICE

PINEAPPLE LEAVES

Method

Blend all ingredients with ice and pour into glass. Garnish with pineapple slice and leaves.

Frangelico, Lime and Soda

GLASS

OLD FASHIONED SPIRIT GLASS

MIXERS

30mL FRANGELICO

15mL LIME CORDIAL

SODA WATER

GARNISH

LIME WEDGE

Method

Build alcohol over ice. Top up with soda water. Garnish with lime wedge to serve.

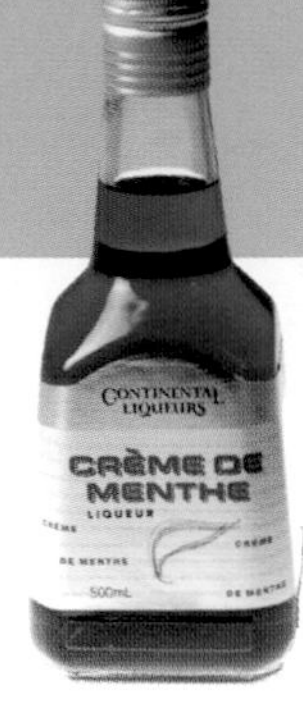

Frappé

Ingredients

GLASS

90mL COCKTAIL GLASS

MIXERS

30mL OF PREFERRED LIQUEUR (e.g., GREEN CRÈME DE MENTHE)

CRUSHED ICE

GARNISH

2 SHORT STRAWS

Method

Build over crushed ice. Garnish with two short straws.

Comments: Spoon the required quantity of crushed ice into the glass. You can create spectacular rainbow effects with small quantities of a range of coloured liqueurs.

Green Crème de Menthe is highly recommended because it acts as a breath freshener when taken after dessert.

Freddy Fudpucker

Ingredients

GLASS

285mL HI-BALL GLASS

MIXERS

30mL TEQUILA

120mL ORANGE JUICE

15mL GALLIANO LIQUEUR

ICE CUBES

GARNISH

1 ORANGE SLICE

1 CHERRY

Method

Build tequila and orange juice over ice. Float in Galliano. Garnish with an orange slice and a cherry. Serve with straws.

French 95

Ingredients

GLASS

135mL TULIP CHAMPAGNE FLUTE

MIXERS

15mL BOURBON OR COGNAC

5mL LEMON JUICE

10mL SUGAR SYRUP

CHAMPAGNE

ICE CUBES

GARNISH

SPIRAL OF LEMON RIND

Method

Shake Bourbon, lemon juice and syrup over ice and strain into glass. Top up with Champagne. Garnish with lemon spiral.

Comments: Substitute gin for Bourbon or cognac to lower the tempo to a French 75.

French Fantasy

Ingredients

GLASS

140mL COCKTAIL GLASS

MIXERS

30mL CRÈME DE GRAND MARNIER

30mL VODKA

15mL TIA MARIA

30mL PINEAPPLE JUICE

30mL ORANGE JUICE

ICE CUBES

GARNISH

BANANA SLICE

RED CHERRY

Method

Shake all ingredients with ice and strain into glass. Garnish with banana slice and red cherry.

Comments: Crème de Grand Marnier is similar to Baileys. This cocktail is really smooth and easy to drink.

Frozen Aquavit

Ingredients

GLASS

90mL COCKTAIL GLASS

MIXERS

45mL AQUAVIT

10mL KIRSCH

10mL LIME JUICE

10mL SUGAR SYRUP

10mL EGG WHITE

CRUSHED ICE

GARNISH

1 COCKTAIL ONION

Method

Blend all ingredients with ice and pour into glass. Garnish with cocktail onion.

Frozen Guava Daiquiri

Ingredients

GLASS

140mL CHAMPAGNE SAUCER

MIXERS

30mL BACARDI RUM

30mL GUAVA NECTAR

15mL LIME JUICE

10mL BANANA LIQUEUR

10mL SUGAR SYRUP

CRUSHED ICE

GARNISH

RED CHERRY

Method

Blend all ingredients with ice and pour into glass. Garnish with red cherry.

Frozen Mudslide

Ingredients

GLASS

290mL POCO GRANDE GLASS

MIXERS

30mL VODKA
20mL BAILEYS IRISH CREAM
20mL KAHLÚA
MILK
WHIPPED CREAM
THICKENED CHOCOLATE
ICE CUBES

GARNISH

STRAWBERRY
HUNDREDS AND THOUSANDS, CONFECTIONERY BALLS

Method

Blend alcohol with ice and pour into glass. Top up with milk then add whipped cream in a swirling motion. With a teaspoon slide in the thickened chocolate (or Ice Magic), thereby creating a Mudslide. Place strawberry on side of glass and sprinkle over hundreds and thousands.

Genoa

Ingredients

GLASS

200mL HI-BALL GLASS

MIXERS

20mL GIN

20mL GRAPPA

10mL SAMBUCA

10mL DRY VERMOUTH

ICE CUBES

GARNISH

OLIVES

Method

Shake all ingredients over ice and strain, then add ice. Garnish with olives.

German Chocolate Cake

Ingredients

GLASS

285mL HURRICANE GLASS

MIXERS

30mL KAHLÚA

30mL MALIBU

30mL CHOCOLATE SYRUP

2 CHOPPED PECAN NUTS

2 scoops VANILLA ICE CREAM

CRUSHED ICE

GARNISH

CHOPPED PECANS

Method

Blend without ice and pour into glass over crushed ice. Garnish with chopped pecans.

Comments: More like a meal than a cocktail! From Germany, a country where eating and drinking are national pastimes, this delicious drink is a gastronomic after-dinner delight.

Gibson

Ingredients

GLASS

90mL COCKTAIL GLASS

MIXERS

60mL GIN

10mL DRY VERMOUTH

GARNISH

1 COCKTAIL ONION

ICE CUBES

Method

Shake over ice and strain into glass. Garnish with one cocktail onion.

Glasgow

Ingredients

GLASS

150mL OLD FASHIONED SPIRIT GLASS

MIXERS

30mL SCOTCH WHISKY

10mL LEMON JUICE

5mL DRY VERMOUTH

5mL ALMOND EXTRACT

ICE CUBES

GARNISH

SLIVERED RAW ALMONDS

DRIED FLOWER OR WHEAT STALK

Method

Shake all ingredients over ice and pour into glass then add ice cube. Garnish with almonds and a dried flower.

Goddaughter

Ingredients

GLASS

140mL CHAMPAGNE SAUCER

MIXERS

30mL SAMBUCA DI GALLIANO

30mL AMARETTO DI GALLIANO

30mL CREAM

5mL GRENADINE CORDIAL

GARNISH

CHOCOLATE FLAKES

1 STRAWBERRY

MINT LEAVES

Method

Shake all ingredients with ice and strain into glass. Garnish with chocolate flakes, strawberry and mint leaves.

Godfather

Ingredients

GLASS

200mL OLD FASHIONED SPIRIT GLASS

MIXERS

30mL SCOTCH WHISKY

30mL AMARETTO DI GALLIANO

ICE CUBES

Method

Build over ice.

Golden Cadillac

Ingredients

GLASS

90mL COCKTAIL GLASS

MIXERS

30mL GALLIANO LIQUEUR

30mL WHITE CRÈME DE CACAO

30mL FRESH CREAM

GARNISH

RED CHERRY OR STRAWBERRY

Method

Shake all ingredients with ice and strain into glass. Garnish with red cherry or strawberry.

Comments: This essence of cocoa beans will take you for the ride of your life. Cruise through this cocktail in luxurious style. Essential for all cocktail parties, anywhere, anytime!

Golden Dream

Ingredients

GLASS

140mL COCKTAIL GLASS

MIXERS

30mL GALLIANO LIQUEUR

20mL COINTREAU

20mL ORANGE JUICE

20mL CREAM

ICE CUBES

GARNISH

ORANGE SLICE

1 STRAWBERRY

Method

Shake all ingredients with ice and strain into glass. Garnish with orange slice and a strawberry on a toothpick on side of glass.

Golden Slipper

Ingredients

GLASS

90mL COCKTAIL GLASS

MIXERS

30mL YELLOW CHARTREUSE

10mL APRICOT BRANDY

1 EGG YOLK

Method

Shake over ice and strain into glass.

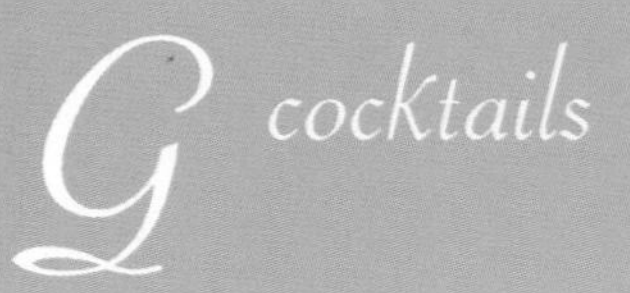

Grasshopper

Ingredients

GLASS

140mL CHAMPAGNE SAUCER

MIXERS

30mL GREEN CRÈME DE MENTHE

30mL WHITE CRÈME DE CACAO

30mL CREAM

CRUSHED ICE

GARNISH

2 RED CHERRIES

Method

Shake all ingredients with ice until smooth and strain into glass. Garnish with two red cherries slit on the side of the glass.

Comments: Jump right into this very popular after-dinner cocktail. Some people prefer Dark Crème de Cacao instead of White Crème de Cacao.

Variations: Add Vodka to create a Flying Grasshopper.

Greenback

Ingredients

GLASS

90mL COCKTAIL GLASS

MIXERS

30mL GIN

10mL LIME JUICE

10mL GREEN CRÈME DE MENTHE

CRACKED ICE

GARNISH

1 LIME SLICE (OPTIONAL)

Method

Stir all ingredients over ice in mixing glass and pour into glass. Garnish with lime slice (optional).

Hair of The Dog

Ingredients

GLASS

210mL OLD FASHIONED SPIRIT GLASS

MIXERS

60mL SCOTCH WHISKY

30mL HONEY

60mL CREAM

ICE CUBES

Method

Fill glass with ice, shake other ingredients and strain over ice into glass. Serve garnished with flower.

Harvey Wallbanger

Ingredients

GLASS

285mL HI-BALL GLASS

MIXERS

40mL VODKA

125mL ORANGE JUICE

15mL GALLIANO LIQUEUR

ICE CUBES

GARNISH

1 ORANGE SLICE

1 CHERRY

Method

Build vodka and orange juice over ice. Float in Galliano. Garnish with orange slice and cherry. Serve with swizzle stick and straws.

Comments: Hawaiian bartenders will tell you a visiting Irishman called Harvey ricocheted down the corridor to his hotel room after a night out. After that he was known as 'Harvey Wallbanger'.

Hawaiian Punch

Ingredients

GLASS

270mL FANCY COCKTAIL GLASS

MIXERS

20mL SOUTHERN COMFORT

20mL AMARETTO DI GALLIANO

15mL VODKA

40mL PINEAPPLE JUICE

40mL ORANGE JUICE

20mL LIME JUICE

20mL GRENADINE CORDIAL

ICE CUBES

GARNISH

THIN WEDGE OF LIME SQUEEZE

THIN WEDGE OF LEMON SQUEEZE

SLICE OF ORANGE

Method

Shake all ingredients except Grenadine over ice and pour. Add Grenadine. Garnish with squeeze of lime juice and lemon juice and slice of orange.

Heartbreaker

Ingredients

GLASS

225mL COLADA GLASS

MIXERS

30mL STRAWBERRY LIQUEUR

60mL CREAM

15mL TIA MARIA

4 STRAWBERRIES

15mL COINTREAU

CRUSHED ICE

GARNISH

STRAWBERRY

Method

Blend until smooth and pour into glass. Serve garnished with strawberry.

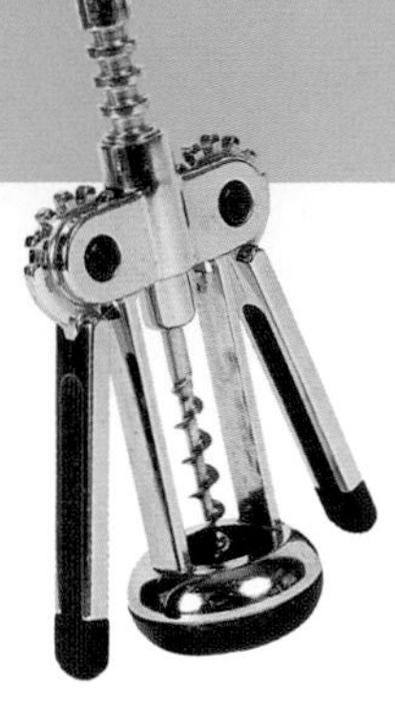

Hellraiser

Ingredients

GLASS

WHISKY SHOT GLASS

MIXERS

10mL RUBIS STRAWBERRY LIQUEUR

10mL MIDORI MELON LIQUEUR

10mL OPAL NERA (SAMBUCA)

Method

Layer in order.

Comments: Shoot this one down – its a hell of a drink!

Hemingway

Ingredients

GLASS

140mL CHAMPAGNE SAUCER

MIXERS

40mL COINTREAU

40mL GRAPEFRUIT JUICE

40mL BACARDI RUM

CRACKED ICE

SPARKLING WHITE WINE

Method

Shake all ingredients with ice except sparkling wine. Strain into a 140mL champagne saucer. Top up with white wine and serve.

Hollywood Nights

Ingredients

GLASS

285mL HI-BALL GLASS

MIXERS

30mL VODKA

15mL PEACH LIQUEUR

10mL MIDORI MELON LIQUEUR

30mL PINEAPPLE JUICE

SODA WATER

CRACKED ICE

Method

Three-quarters fill glass with ice, add vodka, peach liqueur and pineapple juice. Add soda water until 1cm from top. Float Midori, add straws and serve.

Honey Bee

Ingredients

GLASS

145mL COCKTAIL GLASS

MIXERS

30mL BRANDY

15mL HONEY

15mL GALLIANO LIQUEUR

60mL CREAM

15mL GRENADINE CORDIAL

CRACKED ICE

Method

Shake all ingredients vigorously and strain into glass. Serve garnished with flower.

Honey Flow

Ingredients

GLASS

140mL CHAMPAGNE SAUCER

MIXERS

30mL BACARDI RUM

45mL CREAM

15mL GALLIANO LIQUEUR

15mL HONEY

CRACKED ICE

GARNISH

1 MARASCHINO CHERRY

Method

Shake all ingredients and strain into glass. Garnish with cherry and serve.

Horse Guards

Ingredients

GLASS

285mL TUMBLER GLASS

MIXERS

20mL DARK RUM

1 EGG YOLK

20mL COINTREAU

SPARKLING WHITE WINE

3 ICE CUBES

GARNISH

1 SPIRAL LEMON RIND

Method

Shake ingredients except wine. Strain into glass, top up with wine and garnish with lemon rind and serve.

Hot Buttered Rum

Ingredients

GLASS

250mL IRISH COFFEE MUG, PREHEATED

MIXERS

60mL DARK RUM

1 LEMON SLICE

1 CINNAMON STICK

1 CLOVE

APPLE CIDER, WARMED

GARNISH

10mL UNSALTED BUTTER

NUTMEG

Method

Build rum over lemon and spices and top up with warm apple cider. Garnish with butter and nutmeg.

Hot Whiskey Toddy

Ingredients

GLASS

250mL TUMBLER

MIXERS

30mL TULLAMORE DEW IRISH WHISKEY

SUGAR TO TASTE

BOILING WATER

GARNISH

LEMON SLICE

CLOVES

GROUND NUTMEG

Method

Build whiskey over lemon slice studded with cloves and sugar. Top up with boiling water then stir. Garnish with nutmeg. You should pour the whiskey over the lemon slice to bring out the flavour.

Hurricane

Ingredients

GLASS

340mL HURRICANE GLASS

MIXERS

30mL BACARDI RUM

30mL PASSIONFRUIT LIQUEUR

15mL LEMON CORDIAL

45mL LEMON JUICE

45mL SUGAR SYRUP

15mL BACARDI GOLD RUM

CRUSHED ICE

GARNISH

ORANGE SLICE

Method

Shake all ingredients except Bacardi with ice and pour into glass. Float in Bacardi Gold and garnish with orange slice.

COCKTAIL RECIPES
I–M

Ice Kacang

Ingredients

GLASS

350mL TUMBLER GLASS

MIXERS

30mL VODKA

15mL PEACH LIQUEUR

30mL CRANBERRY JUICE

30mL ORANGE JUICE

LEMONADE

DICED FRUIT PIECES

CRUSHED OR SHAVED ICE

Method

Stir ingredients in mixing glass and pour over crushed ice into cooler glass. Serve with two straws and a long spoon.

Comments: Ice or es kacang is known as a dessert from the old Portuguese trading port of Malacca, East Malaysia. This cocktail variation is perfect for hot summer nights.

Independence

Ingredients

GLASS

125mL FANCY COCKTAIL GLASS

MIXERS

30mL BOURBON

15mL LEMON JUICE

15mL BRANDY

60mL ORANGE JUICE

ICE CUBES

GARNISH

1 MINT SPRIG

Method

Shake all ingredients with ice and strain into glass. Garnish with sprig of mint and serve.

Inspiration

Ingredients

GLASS

150mL COCKTAIL GLASS

MIXERS

45mL FRANGELICO

60mL PINEAPPLE JUICE

15mL BANANA LIQUEUR

30mL CREAM

ICE CUBES

GARNISH

STRAWBERRY

MINT LEAF

Method

Shake all ingredients with ice and strain into glass. Garnish with a strawberry and mint leaf on rim and serve.

Intimate

Ingredients

GLASS

90mL COCKTAIL GLASS

MIXERS

20mL VODKA

20mL APRICOT BRANDY

20mL DRY VERMOUTH

ICE CUBES

2 dashes ORANGE BITTERS

GARNISH

1 BLACK OLIVE

1 twist LEMON RIND

Method

Stir all ingredients in mixing glass and strain into cocktail glass. Garnish with olive and lemon rind and serve.

Irish Coffee (Baileys)

Ingredients

GLASS

250mL IRISH COFFEE GLASS

MIXERS

30mL BAILEYS IRISH CREAM

1 teaspoon BROWN SUGAR

HOT BLACK COFFEE

30mL FRESH WHIPPED CREAM

GARNISH

CHOCOLATE FLAKES OR CHOCOLATE POWDER (OPTIONAL)

Method

Stir sugar into Baileys. Top up with coffee. Float fresh cream.

Comments: Baileys Irish Coffee is one of the most popular liqueur coffees. To make Irish coffee with whiskey, substitute a good Irish whiskey such as Tullamore Dew or Jameson's for the Baileys in the recipe above. Other liqueur coffees are: French – Brandy, English – Gin, Russian – Vodka, American – Bourbon, Calypso – Dark Rum, Jamaican – Tia Maria, Parisienne – Grand Marnier, Mexican – Kahlúa, Monks – Benedictine, Scottish – Scotch, Canadian – Rye.

Iron Lady

Ingredients

GLASS

125mL MARGARITA GLASS

MIXERS

15mL MALIBU

45mL CREAM

20mL RUBIS STRAWBERRY LIQUEUR

5mL VANILLA ESSENCE

15mL WHITE CRÈME DE CACAO

1 Scoop VANILLA ICE CREAM

Method

Blend all ingredients until smooth, pour into glass and serve.

Island Cooler

Ingredients

GLASS

140mL CHAMPAGNE SAUCER

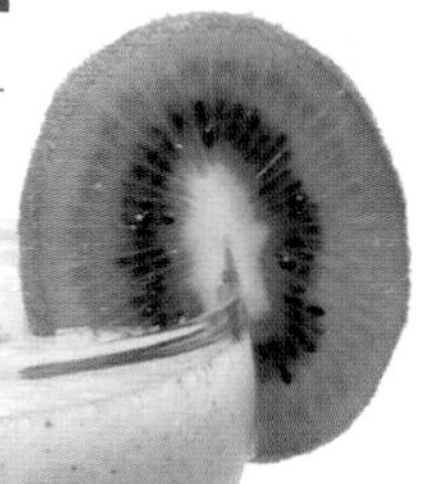

MIXERS

15mL VODKA

30mL ORANGE JUICE

2 scoops CRUSHED ICE

2 drops GRENADINE CORDIAL

30mL MIDORI MELON LIQUEUR

$^{1}/_{4}$ KIWIFRUIT

8mL LEMON JUICE

GARNISH

KIWIFRUIT SLICE

Method

Blend vodka, orange juice and ice until it is a frozen slurry. Pour into champagne saucer then add Grenadine. Blend Midori, kiwifruit and lemon juice and add to glass. Serve garnished with slice of kiwifruit.

Italian Streaker

Ingredients

GLASS

130mL COCKTAIL GLASS

MIXERS

45mL CREAM

15mL GALLIANO LIQUEUR

30mL ANISETTE LIQUEUR

ICE CUBES

GARNISH

ORANGE SLICE

Method

Shake over ice and pour.
Garnish with an orange slice.

Variations: Pernod may be used as a substitute for anisette.

Jelly Bean

Ingredients

GLASS

285mL HI-BALL GLASS

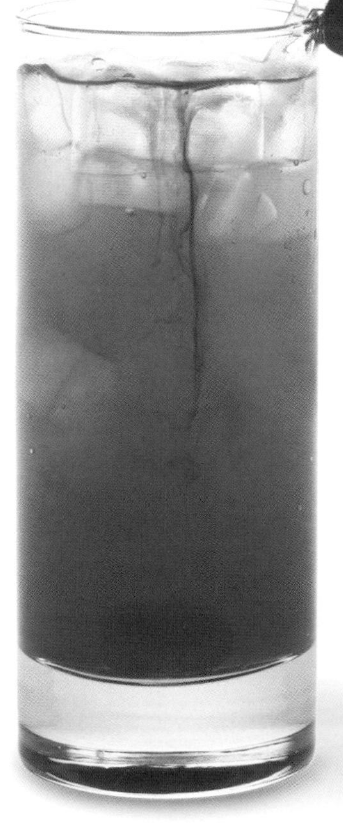

MIXERS

30mL OUZO

15mL BLUE CURAÇAO

15mL GRENADINE CORDIAL

LEMONADE

ICE CUBES

GARNISH

1 RED CHERRY

Method

Build all ingredients except lemonade in glass over ice. Top up with lemonade. Garnish with a swizzle stick and straws and cherry dropped into glass.

Comments: A cool liquid confectionery. Dropping the Blue Curaçao and Grenadine into the cocktail after presenting to the customer, instead of building, gives a swirling lollipop effect. Regularly made without the Blue Curaçao.

Joburg

Ingredients

GLASS

150mL OLD FASHIONED SPIRIT GLASS

MIXERS

30mL BACARDI RUM

15mL DUBONNET

3 dashes ORANGE BITTERS

ICE CUBES

GARNISH

1 twist ORANGE RIND

Method

Shake over ice and strain into glass, then add fresh ice cubes. Garnish with a twist of orange rind.

KGB

Ingredients

GLASS

185mL OLD FASHIONED SPIRIT GLASS

MIXERS

30mL KAHLÚA

30mL GRAND MARNIER

30mL BAILEYS IRISH CREAM

ICE CUBES

Method

Build over ice.

Comments: The first letter of each of the ingredients give this cocktail its name. A late night party drink.

Kakuri

Ingredients

GLASS

90mL COCKTAIL GLASS

MIXERS

30mL PIMM'S NO. 1 CUP

5mL LEMON JUICE

15mL MANGO LIQUEUR

ICE CUBES

15mL BIANCO VERMOUTH

Method

Shake all ingredients and strain into glass. Serve with swizzle stick.

Keep Going

Ingredients

GLASS

285mL FOOTED HI-BALL GLASS

MIXERS

30mL WHITE RUM

15mL GRAPEFRUIT JUICE

15mL PERNOD

30mL COLA TONIC

1/2 slice LEMON

15mL LIME JUICE

CRACKED ICE

LEMONADE

GARNISH

1 slice OF LEMON

Method

Half fill glass with cracked ice, shake ingredients and strain into glass. Serve garnished with slice of lemon and straws.

Kelly's Comfort

Ingredients

GLASS

285mL FOOTED HI-BALL GLASS

MIXERS

30mL SOUTHERN COMFORT

15mL SUGAR SYRUP

30mL BAILEYS IRISH CREAM

3 STRAWBERRIES

60mL MILK

CRUSHED ICE

GARNISH

1 STRAWBERRY

Method

Blend all ingredients until smooth and pour into glass. Serve garnished with strawberry and straws.

Kick in the Balls

Ingredients

GLASS

140mL CHAMPAGNE SAUCER

MIXERS

30mL DARK RUM

30mL ORANGE JUICE

30mL MIDORI MELON LIQUEUR

30mL CREAM

15mL COCONUT CREAM

ICE CUBES

GARNISH

2 MELON BALLS, MARINATED IN THE RUM ABOVE

Method

Shake all ingredients with ice and strain into glass. Garnish with two marinated melon balls.

Comments: Use a toothpick to eat both balls together and you'll be sure to feel a 'Kick in the Balls'. Refrigerate melon balls when marinating to preserve their freshness.

KIR

Ingredients

GLASS

140mL WINE GLASS

MIXERS

15mL CASSIS LIQUEUR

DRY WHITE WINE

Method

Pour cassis liqueur into glass. then top up with dry white wine. No ice.

Comments: A superb pre-dinner drink. Use cold dry wines. Do not spoil the drink by using more than 15mL of Cassis liqueur.

Variations: To make a Kir Imperial substitute 5mL Grenadine for 15mL Cassis. Said to have been named after a former mayor of Dijon, France. Kir Royale is served in a 140mL champagne flute with of 5mL Cassis liqueur topped with the best champagne available. Always remember, the better the champagne, the better the drink.

Hint: With Kir Royale sprinkle a thumb pinch of sugar into glass to produce fizzy bubbles from the white wine. Served chilled.

Klondyke

Ingredients

GLASS

90mL COCKTAIL GLASS

MIXERS

40mL CALVADOS

15mL DRY VERMOUTH

1 dash ANGOSTURA BITTERS

ICE CUBES

GARNISH

1 OLIVE

1 strip LEMON RIND

Method

Mix ingredients in mixing glass and strain into glass. Serve garnished with olive and lemon rind.

Knockout

Ingredients

GLASS

285mL FOOTED PILSENER GLASS

MIXERS

30mL SCOTCH WHISKY

1 EGG YOLK

10mL SUGAR SYRUP

CRACKED ICE

SPARKLING WHITE WINE

GARNISH

1 strip ORANGE RIND

Method

Shake all ingredients except wine and strain into glass. Top up with wine and serve garnished with orange rind.

Lady in Red

Ingredients

GLASS

140mL CHAMPAGNE SAUCER

MIXERS

30mL VODKA

10mL LEMON JUICE

30mL STRAWBERRY LIQUEUR

1 dash EGG WHITE

10mL GRENADINE CORDIAL

4 STRAWBERRIES

1 CRACKED ICE

GARNISH

STRAWBERRY

Method

Blend with ice and pour into a champagne saucer. Serve garnished with strawberry.

Lady Love

Ingredients

GLASS

150mL FANCY COCKTAIL GLASS

MIXERS

30mL VODKA

30mL GALLIANO LIQUEUR

30mL DRY VERMOUTH

30mL ORANGE CURAÇAO

CRACKED ICE

GARNISH

1 twist ORANGE RIND

Method

Shake all ingredients and strain into glass. Garnish with orange rind to serve.

Lady Lynne

Ingredients

GLASS

140mL CHAMPAGNE SAUCER

MIXERS

45mL GIN

10mL LIME JUICE

30mL PARFAIT AMOUR

ICE CUBES

1 dash EGG WHITE

GARNISH

1 STRAWBERRY

Method

Shake all ingredients with ice and strain into champagne saucer. Garnish with strawberry and serve.

Last Emperor

Ingredients

GLASS

140mL FOOTED COCKTAIL GLASS

MIXERS

30mL CANADIAN CLUB RYE WHISKY

30mL BIANCO VERMOUTH

15mL GRAND MARNIER

30mL ORANGE JUICE

1 dash ANGOSTURA BITTERS

CRACKED ICE

GARNISH

1 strip ORANGE RIND

Method

Pour all ingredients into glass over ice. Add strip of orange rind and serve.

Lena

Ingredients

GLASS

140mL COCKTAIL GLASS

MIXERS

60mL BOURBON

15mL CAMPARI

30mL ROSSO VERMOUTH

15mL GALLIANO LIQUEUR

15mL DRY VERMOUTH

ICE CUBES

GARNISH

1 MARASCHINO CHERRY

Method

Stir all ingredients over ice in mixing glass and strain into glass. Garnish with cherry and serve.

Leprechaun

Ingredients

GLASS

210mL OLD FASHIONED SPIRITED GLASS

MIXERS

60mL TULLAMORE DEW IRISH WHISKEY

180mL TONIC WATER

GARNISH

LIME SLICE

Method

Build over ice. Garnish with a lime slice dropped into the glass.

Lights of Havana

Ingredients

GLASS

275mL HI-BALL GLASS

MIXERS

60mL SODA WATER

40mL MALIBU

25mL MIDORI MELON LIQUEUR

60mL ORANGE JUICE

60mL PINEAPPLE JUICE

ICE CUBES

GARNISH

LIME WHEEL

Method

Shake all ingredients over ice and pour into glass. Garnish with a straw and a lime wheel.

London Fog

Ingredients

GLASS

90mL COCKTAIL GLASS

MIXERS

10mL WHITE CRÈME DE MENTHE

5mL ANISETTE LIQUEUR

2 dashes ANGOSTURA BITTERS

ICE CUBES

GARNISH

MINT SPRIG

Method

Stir in mixing glass with over ice and strain into cocktail glass. Garnish with a mint sprig.

Comments: Anisette liqueur is a French brand of liquorice-flavoured liqueur made from anise seed. Pernod may be substituted.

Long Island Iced Tea

Ingredients

GLASS

285mL HI-BALL GLASS

MIXERS

30mL TEQUILA

30mL GIN

30mL VODKA

30mL BACARDI RUM

30mL COINTREAU

30mL LEMON JUICE

15mL COLA (TO COLOUR ONLY)

ICE CUBES

GARNISH

1 twist LEMON RIND

MINT LEAVES

Method

Build in the glass and stir. Garnish with a lemon twist and mint leaves.

Long Neck

Ingredients

GLASS

285mL OLD FASHIONED SPIRIT GLASS

MIXERS

45mL VODKA

30mL MIDORI MELON LIQUEUR

1 scoop CRUSHED ICE

30mL LEMON JUICE

1 dash GRENADINE CORDIAL

Method

Blend all ingredients except Grenadine until frozen, place in glass. Add Grenadine and serve.

Love Potion Number 9

Ingredients

GLASS

140mL CHAMPAGNE SAUCER

MIXERS

60mL BACARDI RUM

1/2 EGG WHITE

30mL COINTREAU

CRACKED ICE

15mL LEMON JUICE

GARNISH

1 MARASCHINO CHERRY (OPTIONAL)

Method

Shake all ingredients and strain into champagne saucer. Garnish with cherry and serve.

Lover

Ingredients

GLASS

140mL FANCY COCKTAIL GLASS

MIXERS

60mL SCOTCH WHISKY

30mL CAMPARI

30mL BIANCO VERMOUTH

CRACKED ICE

GARNISH

1 twist ORANGE RIND

Method

Shake all ingredients and strain into a fancy cocktail glass. Garnish with orange rind and serve.

Lucky Dip

Ingredients

GLASS

140mL FANCY COCKTAIL GLASS

MIXERS

60mL VODKA

1/2 EGG WHITE

30mL CRÈME DE BANANA

30mL LEMON SQUASH

CRACKED ICE

GARNISH

LEMON WHEEL

Method

Shake all ingredients and strain into a fancy cocktail glass. Serve garnished with wheel of lemon.

Lynchburg Lemonade

Ingredients

GLASS

285mL HI-BALL GLASS

MIXERS

20mL JACK DANIEL'S TENNESSE WHISKEY

20mL COINTREAU

20mL FRESH LIME JUICE

LEMONADE OR SODA WATER

GARNISH

1 strip LEMON PEEL

Method

Pour in order then top up with lemonade or soda water. Serve garnished with twisted lemon rind.

Comments: This delicious cocktail originates from the home of Jack Daniel's.

Machine Gun Kelly

Ingredients

GLASS

140mL CHAMPAGNE SAUCER

MIXERS

45mL SCOTCH WHISKY

1 dash ORANGE BITTERS

30mL SWEET VERMOUTH

30mL DRY VERMOUTH

CRACKED ICE

GARNISH

1 twist LEMON RIND

Method

Shake all ingredients and strain into champagne saucer. Garnish with lemon rind and serve.

Madame Butterfly

Ingredients

GLASS

180mL MARGARITA GLASS

MIXERS 1

30mL PASSIONFRUIT LIQUEUR (OR 1/2 PASSIONFRUIT)

15mL MIDORI MELON LIQUEUR

15mL WHITE CRÈME DE CACAO

30mL PINEAPPLE JUICE

CRACKED ICE

MIXERS 2

30mL CREAM

15mL MIDORI MELON LIQUEUR

GARNISH

1 STRAWBERRY

BUTTERFLY ORNAMENT

Method

Shake passionfruit liqueur, Midori, Crème de Cacao and pineapple juice with ice and strain into glass. Shake Midori and cream, then float into glass. Garnish with strawberry and butterfly ornament.

Madras

Ingredients

GLASS

170mL TULIP CHAMPAGNE FLUTE

MIXERS

30mL VODKA

80mL CRANBERRY JUICE

30mL ORANGE JUICE

CRUSHED ICE

Method

Build vodka and cranberry juice over ice float in orange juice to top up.

Malibu Magic

Ingredients

GLASS

285mL FOOTED HI-BALL GLASS

MIXERS

30mL MALIBU

5 STRAWBERRIES

30mL STRAWBERRY LIQUEUR

60mL CREAM

30mL ORANGE JUICE

CRACKED ICE

GARNISH

1 STRAWBERRY

Method

Blend all ingredients and pour into glass. Garnish with strawberry and straws, and serve.

Mama Rosa

Ingredients

GLASS

300mL FOOTED PILSENER GLASS

MIXERS

30mL SAMBUCA

30mL CHERRY ADVOCAAT

SODA WATER

ICE CUBES

GARNISH

MARASCHINO CHERRY

PINEAPPLE LEAVES

ORANGE SLICE

Method

Build Sambuca and Advocaat over ice then top up with soda water. Garnish with maraschino cherry, pineapple leaves and orange slice.

Mandarin Sling

Ingredients

GLASS

140mL CHAMPAGNE SAUCER

MIXERS

20mL KAHLÚA

20mL DARK CRÈME DE CACAO

10mL CHOCOLATE SYRUP

2 scoops ORANGE SORBET

½ MANDARIN

GARNISH

SLICE OF MANDARIN OR ORANGE

Method

Blend all ingredients without ice. Garnish with a mandarin or orange slice.

Comments: At the Mandarin Hotel in Orchard Road, Singapore, this citrus-based cocktail is a favourite.

Manhattan

Ingredients

GLASS

90mL COCKTAIL GLASS

MIXERS

30mL BOURBON

15mL ROSSO VERMOUTH

dash ANGOSTURA BITTERS

GARNISH

RED CHERRY

Method

Stir all ingredients over ice and strain into glass. Garnish with a red cherry on toothpick in glass.

Comments: A pre-dinner cocktail. Frequently served to overseas guests, particularly New Yorkers.

Variations: Replace Rosso Vermouth with Cinzano Dry, add a twist of lemon and you have instantly mixed a Dry Manhattan.

Rye Whiskey may be substituted for Bourbon.

Margarita (assorted)

Ingredients

GLASS

350mL MARGARITA GLASS, SALT-FROSTED

MIXERS

30mL LIQUEUR TO MATCH FRUIT AVAILABLE (MIDORI, RUBIS, LENA, MOHALA)

30mL TEQUILA

45mL LEMON JUICE

15mL LIME CORDIAL OR SUGAR SYRUP

2–3 pieces OF FRUIT TO MATCH LIQUEUR (HONEYDEW MELON, STRAWBERRY, BANANA, MANGO)

CRACKED ICE

GARNISH

LEMON WHEEL

Method

Blend all ingredients with ice. Pour into salt-frosted glass. Serve garnished with wheel of lemon.

Martini

Ingredients

GLASS

90mL COCKTAIL GLASS

MIXERS

45mL GIN

20mL DRY VERMOUTH

ICE CUBES

GARNISH

twist OF LEMON RIND OR OLIVE

Method

Stir all ingredients over ice and strain. Garnish with lemon twist or olive on toothpick in the glass.

Comments: The classically sophisticated black-tie cocktail. Always stirred. However, when shaken it is known as a 'Bradford'. An olive garnish retains the gin sting whereas a lemon twist makes the cocktail smoother.

Variations: A 'Dry Martini' has less Vermouth.

Ménage à Trois

Ingredients

GLASS

285mL HURRICANE GLASS

MIXERS

30mL PERNOD

30mL MALIBU

60mL PINEAPPLE JUICE

15mL COCONUT CREAM

1 scoop ORANGE SORBET

1 scoop VANILLA ICE CREAM

ICE CUBES

GARNISH

1 STRAWBERRY

PINEAPPLE LEAVES

Method

Blend and pour into glass. Garnish with a strawberry, pineapple leaves and three straws.

Comments: Voulez vous coucher avec moi ce soir? When two's not enough company try this drink that originated from the afternoon cocktail parties held on the crowded houseboats lining the River Seine in Paris. Ideal for three people.

Mexican Flag

Ingredients

GLASS

140mL CHAMPAGNE SAUCER

MIXERS

60mL TEQUILA

10mL SUGAR SYRUP

10mL LIME JUICE

ICE CUBES

GARNISH

1 GREEN COCKTAIL ONION

1 WHITE COCKTAIL ONION

1 RED CHERRY

ICE CUBES

Method

Shake all ingredients over ice and pour into glass. Garnish with green and white cocktail onions and a red cherry across the glass on a toothpick.

Mexican Runner

Ingredients

GLASS

300mL FANCY COCKTAIL GLASS

MIXERS

30mL TEQUILA

15mL TIA MARIA

15mL GRAND MARNIER

15mL BLACKBERRY LIQUEUR

30mL LEMON JUICE

$^1/_2$ BANANA

2 STRAWBERRIES

CRACKED ICE

GARNISH

1 STRAWBERRY

Method

Blend all over ice and pour into glass. Garnish with a strawberry and umbrella parasol.

Midnight Sax

Ingredients

GLASS

450mL TUMBLER GLASS

MIXERS

30mL MIDORI MELON LIQUEUR

30mL SOUTHERN COMFORT

30mL ORANGE AND MANGO FRUIT JUICES

GINGER ALE

ICE CUBES

GARNISH

ORANGE SLICE

twist OF ORANGE RIND

Method

Pour all ingredients except ginger ale into glass over ice and stir, then top up with ginger ale. Garnish with slices of orange in the glass and orange twist on the side.

Comments: Jazz is the music of the moods. Experience this fiery, and soulful music with this unique cocktail, rumoured to be one of Charlie Parker's former favourites.

Midori Illusion

Ingredients

GLASS

145mL COCKTAIL GLASS

MIXERS

30mL MIDORI MELON LIQUEUR

15mL COINTREAU

15mL VODKA

45mL LEMON JUICE

15mL LIME CORDIAL OR SUGAR SYRUP

ICE CUBES

GARNISH

LIME WHEEL

Method

Shake all ingredients with ice and strain into glass. Serve garnished with lime wheel.

Midori Pash

Ingredients

GLASS

270mL FOOTED HI-BALL GLASS

MIXERS

60mL MIDORI MELON LIQUEUR

30mL VODKA

15mL LIME CORDIAL

CRANBERRY JUICE

ICE CUBES

GARNISH

ORANGE WHEEL

Method

Shake ingredients and strain into glass over ice. Serve garnished with wheel of orange.

Midori Splice

Ingredients

GLASS

270mL HI-BALL GLASS

MIXERS

30mL MIDORI MELON LIQUEUR

30mL MALIBU

PINEAPPLE JUICE

15mL FRESH CREAM

ICE CUBES

GARNISH

PINEAPPLE WEDGE

Method

Build Midori, Malibu and juice over ice. Float in cream

Comments: A Midori Splice can also be served in a tulip glass

Mint Julep

Ingredients

GLASS

285mL HI-BALL TOM COLLINS GLASS

MIXERS

1 teaspoon SUGAR

2–3 dashes COLD WATER OR SODA WATER

5 sprigs FRESH MINT

60mL BOURBON

CRUSHED OR SHAVED ICE

GARNISH

3 MINT SPRIGS, SUGAR-FROSTED

Method

Muddle sugar, water and 5 mint sprigs in a glass. Pour into thoroughly chilled glass and pack with ice. Add bourbon and mix with a chopping motion using a long-handled bar spoon. Garnish with remaining mint and serve with a straw.

Comments: Tear mint leaves slightly before frosting in sugar for greater aroma and flavour.

Monte Carlo

Ingredients

GLASS

90mL COCKTAIL GLASS

MIXERS

30mL CANADIAN CLUB RYE WHISKY

10mL BENEDICTINE

2 dashes ANGOSTURA BITTERS

ICE CUBES

Method

Shake all ingredients with ice and strain into glass.

Morning Glory

Ingredients

GLASS

150mL OLD FASHIONED SPIRIT GLASS

MIXERS

30mL SCOTCH WHISKY

30mL BRANDY

5mL PERNOD

5mL WHITE CURAÇAO

2 dashes ANGOSTURA BITTERS

SODA WATER

ICE CUBES

GARNISH

1 twist ORANGE RIND

Method

Shake all ingredients except soda water with ice and pour then top up with soda water. Garnish with orange twist.

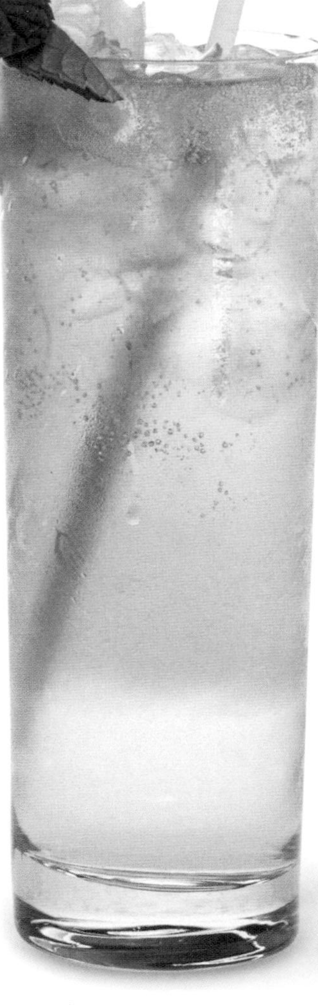

Moscow Mule

Ingredients

GLASS

285mL HI-BALL GLASS

MIXERS

30mL VODKA

15mL LIME CORDIAL

GINGER BEER

ICE CUBES

GARNISH

1 LEMON SLICE

1 MINT SPRIG

Method

Build in glass over ice. Garnish with a slice of lemon and mint, straws and a swizzle stick.

Mount Fuji

Ingredients

GLASS

90mL COCKTAIL GLASS

MIXERS

30mL GIN

15mL LEMON JUICE

10mL DOUBLE CREAM

1 EGG WHITE

ICE CUBES

GARNISH

RED CHERRY

Method

Shake all ingredients with ice and strain into glass. Serve garnished with a red cherry.

COCKTAIL RECIPES

M–R

Napoleon Seduction

Ingredients

GLASS

125mL FOOTED HI-BALL GLASS

MIXERS

15mL MANGO LIQUEUR

30mL CREAM

30mL MANDARIN NAPOLEON

20g MANGO

15mL SABRA

CRACKED ICE

GARNISH

1 MARASCHINO CHERRY

ORANGE WHEEL

Method

Blend all the ingredients with ice until smooth. Pour into a glass. Garnish with cherry and orange wheel, and serve.

New Yorker

Ingredients

GLASS

90mL COCKTAIL GLASS

MIXERS

15mL GIN

1 dash COINTREAU

45mL DRY VERMOUTH

CRACKED ICE

15mL SWEET SHERRY

GARNISH

ORANGE RIND

Method

Stir all ingredients in mixing glass and strain into glass to serve.

Night of Passion

Ingredients

GLASS

270mL FANCY ROCKS GLASS

MIXERS

60mL GIN

15mL LEMON JUICE

30mL COINTREAU

60mL PASSIONFRUIT JUICE

60mL PEACH NECTAR

CRACKED ICE

Method

Shake all ingredients and strain into glass to serve.

NOAH'S ARK

Ingredients

GLASS

37mL CORDIAL GLASS (LEXINGTON)

MIXERS

10mL BLUE CURAÇAO

10mL CREAM

10mL LEMONADE

GARNISH

½ LYCHEE NUT (OPTIONAL)

Method

Shake Blue Curaçao with cream, then float in lemonade. Optionally, place half a lychee nut in glass before pouring.

Norman Conquest

Ingredients

GLASS

90mL FANCY COCKTAIL GLASS

MIXERS

60mL CALVADOS

1 teaspoon GRENADINE CORDIAL

2 tablespoon LEMON JUICE

CRACKED ICE

GARNISH

1 LIME WHEEL

Method

Shake all ingredients and strain into glass. Serve garnished with lime wheel.

Nutcracker

Ingredients

GLASS

270mL HI-BALL GLASS

MIXERS

30mL FRANGELICO

30mL DARK RUM

60mL CLOUDY APPLE JUICE

10mL FRESH LIME JUICE

1 dash ANGOSTURA BITTERS

6 MINT LEAVES

CRACKED ICE

GARNISH

1 APPLE SLICE

1 MINT SPRIG

Method

Shake all ingredients and strain over ice into glass. Garnish with an apple slice and a mint sprig.

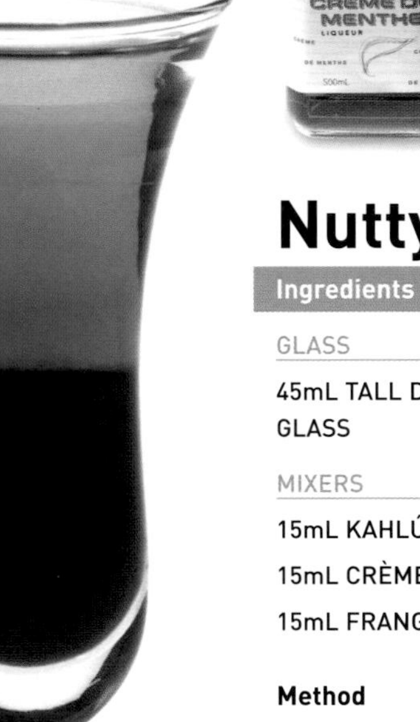

Nutty Buddy

Ingredients

GLASS

45mL TALL DUTCH CORDIAL GLASS

MIXERS

15mL KAHLÚA

15mL CRÈME DE MENTHE

15mL FRANGELICO

Method

Layer in order.

Comment: Customers should shoot back this crazy cocktail.

Nutty Irishman

Ingredients

GLASS

IRISH COFFEE GLASS

MIXERS

30mL FRANGELICO

30mL BAILEYS IRISH CREAM

60mL CREAM

GARNISH

CHOCOLATE FLAKES

Method

Shake all ingredients into glass and strain. Serve garnished with chocolate flakes.

Oatmeal Cookie

Ingredients

GLASS

90mL COCKTAIL GLASS

MIXERS

30mL JÄGERMEISTER

15mL BAILEYS IRISH CREAM

15mL BUTTERSCOTCH SCHNAPPS

30mL CREAM

ICE CUBES

GARNISH

CHOCOLATE SPRINKLES

Method

Shake all ingredients with ice and strain into glass. Serve garnished with chocolate sprinkles.

Oceanic

Ingredients

GLASS

140mL CHAMPAGNE FLUTE

MIXERS

45mL SCOTCH WHISKY

15mL BIANCO VERMOUTH

30mL KAHLÚA

CRACKED ICE

GARNISH

1 ORANGE RIND

Method

Mix all ingredients in a mixing glass and strain into champagne flute. Garnish with a spiral of orange peel and serve.

Off the Leash

Ingredients

GLASS

140mL CHAMPAGNE SAUCER

MIXERS

90mL BRANDY

30mL SWEET VERMOUTH

CRACKED ICE

GARNISH

3 MARASCHINO CHERRIES

Method

Mix all ingredients in a mixing glass and strain into glass. Garnish with maraschino cherries and serve.

Old-Fashioned Appetiser

Ingredients

GLASS

150mL OLD FASHIONED SPIRIT GLASS

MIXERS

1 CUBE OF ICE

20mL BOURBON

20mL DUBONNET

5mL COINTREAU

5mL PERNOD

1 dash ANGOSTURA BITTERS

GARNISH

LEMON RIND

ORANGE RIND

Method

Build over ice. Garnish with lemon and orange rind.

Old-Fashioned Scotch

Ingredients

GLASS

285mL OLD FASHIONED SPIRIT GLASS

MIXERS

30mL SCOTCH WHISKY

1 dash ANGOSTURA BITTERS

SUGAR CUBE

SODA WATER

GARNISH

½ slice ORANGE

½ slice LEMON

1 CHERRY

Method

Build scotch and bitters over ice and sugar cubes. Top up with soda water. Garnish with ½ slice of orange and lemon and cherry. A swizzle stick may be used.

Comment: The origin of this cocktail is uncertain, however, some say it was invented at the Pendennis Club, Louisville, Kentucky, in the 1880s, as the result of the bar staff being asked for a 'good old fashioned cocktail'.

Orangutan

Ingredients

GLASS

270mL FANCY COCKTAIL GLASS

MIXERS

30mL MIDORI MELON LIQUEUR

90mL ORANGE JUICE

30mL MANDARIN NAPOLEON

90mL PINEAPPLE JUICE

CRACKED ICE

GARNISH

2 ORANGE SLICES

PINEAPPLE LEAVES

Method

Half fill a cocktail glass with ice and build ingredients. Garnish with orange slices, pineapple leaves and straws to serve.

Orgasm

Ingredients

GLASS

210mL OLD FASHIONED SPIRIT GLASS

MIXERS

30mL BAILEYS IRISH CREAM

30mL COINTREAU

ICE CUBES

GARNISH

STRAWBERRY OR CHERRIES

Method

Build over ice.

Comments: Probably the most widely drunk cocktail in Australia and very popular with women.

Variations: A 'Multiple Orgasm' is made with the addition of 30mL of fresh cream or milk.

A 'Screaming Multiple Orgasm' has the addition of 15mL Galliano along with 30mL fresh cream or milk.

Oriental Blossom

Ingredients

GLASS

225mL COLADA GLASS

MIXERS

30mL BANANA LIQUEUR

90mL APPLE JUICE

30mL SOUTHERN COMFORT

30mL FRESH CREAM

15mL RED CURAÇAO

2 APPLE SLICES

ICE CUBES

GARNISH

APPLE SLICES

Method

Shake all ingredients with ice and strain into glass. Garnish with apple slices and serve.

Oriental Pearl

Ingredients

GLASS

140mL CHAMPAGNE SAUCER

MIXERS

20mL WHITE RUM
15mL FRESH CREAM
10mL CRÈME DE CASSIS
CRACKED ICE
15mL COLA SYRUP

GARNISH

MINT SPRIG

Method

Shake with ice and strain into glass. Serve garnished with mint sprig.

Pablo

Ingredients

GLASS

145mL COCKTAIL GLASS

MIXERS

30mL BACARDI RUM

15mL COINTREAU

15mL ADVOCAAT

CRACKED ICE

GARNISH

1 slice PINEAPPLE

1 MARASCHINO CHERRY

Method

Shake all ingredients with ice and strain into glass. Garnish with pineapple and cherry to serve.

Pago Pago

Ingredients

GLASS

250mL OLD FASHIONED SPIRIT GLASS

MIXERS

30mL BACARDI GOLD RUM

10mL LIME JUICE

10mL PINEAPPLE JUICE

5mL GREEN CHARTREUSE

5mL COINTREAU

ICE CUBES

GARNISH

1 PINEAPPLE WEDGE

1 CHERRY

Method

Shake all ingredients with ice and strain into glass over 3 cubes of ice. Garnish with a pineapple wedge and a cherry to serve

Palm Sundae

Ingredients

GLASS

285mL HURRICANE GLASS

MIXERS

45mL PEACH LIQUEUR

30mL MALIBU

15mL BANANA LIQUEUR

60mL TROPICAL FRUIT JUICE

3 FRESH STRAWBERRIES

CRACKED ICE

GARNISH

1 ORANGE WEDGE

2 PINEAPPLE LEAVES

1 MARASCHINO CHERRY

Method

Blend all ingredients with ice and pour into glass. Garnish with orange wedge, pineapple leaves and maraschino cherry.

Comments: The peach flavour is exquisite in this specially designed cocktail recipe. The succulent peach liqueur is another member of the new generation of natural tropical fruit cocktails.

Papaya Sling

Ingredients

GLASS

285mL HI-BALL GLASS

MIXERS

30mL GIN

15mL LIME JUICE

20mL PAPAYA JUICE OR SYRUP

2 dashes ANGOSTURA BITTERS

SODA WATER

CRACKED ICE

GARNISH

LIME WHEEL

Method

Shake all ingredients with ice and pour into glass. Then top up with soda water. Garnish with a lime wheel.

Peach Almond Shake

Ingredients

GLASS

295mL POCO GRANDE GLASS

MIXERS

60mL PEACH LIQUEUR

1 WHOLE PEELED PEACH

30mL AMARETTO DI GALLIANO

2 scoops VANILLA ICE CREAM

LEMONADE

CRACKED ICE

GARNISH

1 PEACH SLICE

SLIVERED ALMONDS

Method

Blend all ingredients with ice and pour into glass. Then top up with lemonade. Garnish with a peach slice, almonds and a straw.

Peppermint Breeze

Ingredients

GLASS

285mL HI-BALL GLASS

MIXERS

60mL SCOTCH WHISKY

FRESHLY SQUEEZED JUICE OF 1 LIME QUARTER

SODA WATER

BROWN SUGAR LUMP INFUSED WITH 4 DROPS PEPPERMINT ESSENCE

CRACKED ICE

GARNISH

FRESH MINT

Method

Build with cracked ice and add freshly squeezed lime juice. Top up with soda water and stir well. Serve garnished with fresh mint.

Comments: The fresh and reviving flavours of peppermint and lime mixed with the rich, honeyed taste of Scotch Whisky create a delicious, invigorating drink.

Picadilly Punch

Ingredients

GLASS

90mL COCKTAIL GLASS, PREHEATED

MIXERS

30mL COGNAC

10mL SUGAR

15mL LEMON JUICE

1 clove CINNAMON STICK

GROUND NUTMEG

GARNISH

1 ORANGE SLICE

1 RED CHERRY

Method

Simmer all ingredients except for Cognac. Pour Cognac into ladle and ignite before mixing into the punch mix. Stir and pour into preheated glass. Serve garnished with an orange slice and a red cherry.

Picasso

Ingredients

GLASS

90mL COCKTAIL GLASS

MIXERS

30mL COGNAC

10mL DUBONNET

10mL LIME JUICE

15mL SUGAR SYRUP

ICE CUBES

GARNISH

1 twist ORANGE RIND

Method

Shake all ingredients over ice and strain into glass. Garnish with orange twist.

Pimm's No. 1 Cup

Ingredients

GLASS

285mL HI-BALL GLASS

MIXERS

30–45mL PIMM'S NO. 1 CUP

LEMONADE OR DRY GINGER ALE

ICE CUBES

GARNISH

ORANGE SLICE

CHERRY

CUCUMBER (SKIN ON)

Method

Build Pimm's over ice. Top-up with either lemonade or dry ginger or equal parts of both. Garnish with an orange slice, cherry, cucumber skin, swizzle stick and straws.

Comments: A slice of orange can detract from the sweet aftertaste. Slicing the inside of the cucumber skin allows the small drops to keep the drink chilled. Originally six types of Pimm's were commonly consumed, today there are only two: Pimm's No.1, which has a gin base, and Pimm's No. 2, which has a vodka base. Often referred to as the 'Fruit Cocktail Cocktail'.

Pina Colada

Ingredients

GLASS

285mL HI-BALL GLASS

MIXERS

30mL BACARDI RUM

30mL COCONUT CREAM

30mL SUGAR SYRUP

125mL UNSWEETENED PINEAPPLE JUICE

ICE CUBES

GARNISH

1 PINEAPPLE WEDGE

3 PINEAPPLE LEAVES

Method

Shake all ingredients with ice and pour into glass. Garnish with a pineapple wedge, pineapple leaves, straws and swizzle stick.

Comments: A tropical Hawaiian cocktail which is distinguished by including coconut cream.

Pineapple Plantation

Ingredients

GLASS

285mL FOOTED HI-BALL GLASS

MIXERS

30mL AMARETTO DI GALLIANO

30mL SOUTHERN COMFORT

90mL PINEAPPLE JUICE

LEMONADE

CRACKED ICE

GARNISH

1 PINEAPPLE WEDGE

1 CHERRY

Method

Blend all ingredients except lemonade with ice and pour into glass. Then top up with lemonade. Garnish with pineapple wedge and cherry.

Pink Gin

Ingredients

GLASS

285mL HURRICANE GLASS

MIXERS

3 dashes ANGOSTURA BITTERS

2 ICE CUBES

45mL GIN

30mL WATER

GARNISH

1 LEMON SLICE

1 CHERRY

Method

Put bitters into glass. Rotate in the glass, then throw out the bitters. Add ice cubes, gin and water, and serve.

Pink Panther

Ingredients

GLASS

140mL CHAMPAGNE SAUCER

MIXERS

20mL BOURBON

30mL VODKA

15mL MALIBU

40mL CREAM

1 dash GRENADINE CORDIAL

GARNISH

1 CHERRY

MINT LEAF

Method

Shake all ingredients with ice and strain into glass. Garnish with cherry and mint.

Polynesia

Ingredients

GLASS

135mL TULIP CHAMPAGNE FLUTE

MIXERS

30mL BACARDI RUM

30mL PASSIONFRUIT LIQUEUR OR 1/2 PASSIONFRUIT

10mL LIME JUICE

1/2 EGG WHITE

CRACKED ICE

GARNISH

PASSIONFRUIT

Method

Blend all ingredients with ice and pour into glass. Garnish with passionfruit.

Prairie Oyster

Ingredients

GLASS

90mL COCKTAIL GLASS

MIXERS

30mL BRANDY

SALT AND PEPPER

1 dash WORCESTERSHIRE SAUCE

1 dash TABASCO SAUCE

1 EGG YOLK

Method

Build ingredients in order, no ice.

Comments: The spices relieve a sore head and the brandy replenishes lost energy. Brandy may be replaced with any spirit of your choice, however cold vodka is medically soothing. Best before breakfast.

Pretty Woman

Ingredients

GLASS

285mL HURRICANE GLASS

MIXERS – BLEND 1

30mL MIDORI MELON LIQUEUR

30mL MALIBU

MIXERS – BLEND 2

30mL STRAWBERRY LIQUEUR

3–4 STRAWBERRIES

CRACKED ICE

GARNISH

1 STRAWBERRY

Method

Blend with ice in two separate blenders and pour into glass. Tilt the glass when pouring the two sets of ingredients into the glass. Garnish with strawberry and umbrella to serve.

GARNISH

1 ORANGE SLICE

Method

Shake all ingredients except Champagne with ice and strain. Then top up with Champagne. Garnish with orange slice.

Prince of Wales

Ingredients

GLASS

140mL CHAMPAGNE SAUCER

MIXERS

15mL MADEIRA

15mL BRANDY

5mL COINTREAU

1–2 dashes ANGOSTURA BITTERS

CHAMPAGNE

ICE CUBES

Puerto Rican Pink Lady

Ingredients

GLASS

135mL TULIP CHAMPAGNE FLUTE, SUGAR-FROSTED

MIXERS

30mL BACARDI GOLD RUM

10mL LEMON JUICE

10mL GRENADINE CORDIAL

1/2 EGG WHITE

CRACKED ICE

GARNISH

1 STRAWBERRY

Method

Blend all ingredients with ice and pour into glass. Garnish with a strawberry splashed with Grenadine.

Puerto Rico Rickey (picture on cover)

Ingredients

GLASS

285mL HI-BALL GLASS

MIXERS

60mL GIN

30mL LIME JUICE

ICE CUBES

2 dashes RASPBERRY SYRUP

SODA WATER

GARNISH

LIME WHEEL

Method

Pour gin and lime juice over ice into glass. Add the raspberry syrup and top up with soda water. Garnish with a wheel of lime to serve.

Comments: Bourbon, rum or whisky can be substituted for gin.

Purple People Eater

Ingredients

GLASS

90mL COCKTAIL GLASS

MIXERS

30mL PARFAIT AMOUR

30mL GIN

5mL LEMON JUICE

ICE CUBES

GARNISH

1 STRAWBERRY

Method

Shake all ingredients over ice and strain into glass. Garnish with a strawberry and pink parasol to serve.

QF

Ingredients

GLASS

SHOT GLASS

MIXERS

10mL KAHLÚA

10mL MIDORI MELON LIQUEUR

10mL BAILEYS IRISH CREAM

Method

Layer in order.

Queens

Ingredients

GLASS

145mL TULIP CHAMPAGNE FLUTE

MIXERS

30mL DRY GIN

30mL PINEAPPLE JUICE

30mL DRY VERMOUTH

30mL SWEET VERMOUTH (BIANCO)

CRACKED ICE

GARNISH

1 MARASCHINO CHERRY

1 PINEAPPLE WEDGE

Method

Shake all ingredients with ice and strain into glass. Garnish with cherry, pineapple wedge to serve.

R&R

Ingredients

GLASS

90mL FANCY COCKTAIL GLASS

MIXERS

30mL COINTREAU

30mL MIDORI MELON LIQUEUR

30mL TEQUILA

Method

Layer in order in glass and serve.

Rabbit's Revenge

Ingredients

GLASS

140mL FANCY COCKTAIL GLASS

MIXERS

40mL BOURBON

3 dashes GRENADINE CORDIAL

30mL PINEAPPLE JUICE

CRACKED ICE

TONIC WATER

GARNISH

1 ORANGE SLICE

Method

Shake ingredients except tonic water and strain into a tumbler glass. Top up with tonic water and garnish with orange slice to serve.

Rainbow Sherbet

Ingredients

GLASS

195mL TULIP CHAMPAGNE FLUTE

MIXERS

15mL MIDORI MELON LIQUEUR

15mL BANANA LIQUEUR

15mL STRAWBERRY LIQUEUR

60mL ORANGE JUICE

2 dashes GRENADINE CORDIAL

2 scoops ORANGE SORBET

GARNISH

ASSORTED FRUIT

BLUE FOOD COLOURING

Method

Blend all ingredients without ice. Pour into glass. Garnish with assorted fruit and a dash of blue food colouring.

Ramona

Ingredients

GLASS

285mL HI-BALL GLASS

MIXERS

60mL BACARDI RUM

2 teaspoons CASTER SUGAR

30mL COINTREAU

60mL LEMON JUICE

CRACKED ICE

SODA WATER

GARNISH

1 LEMON WHEEL

Method

Shake all ingredients except soda water and strain over ice into glass. Top up with soda water, garnish with lemon wheel and straws to serve.

Red Eye

Ingredients

GLASS

285mL HI-BALL GLASS

MIXERS

140mL COLD BEER

140mL TOMATO JUICE

GARNISH

1/2 CHERRY TOMATO

Method

Pour tomato juice into glass, add beer and serve.

Reflections

Ingredients

GLASS

90mL MARTINI GLASS

MIXERS

30mL FRANGELICO

CRACKED ICE

30mL WHITE CRÈME DE CACAO

15mL CHERI-SUISSE

GARNISH

2 MARASCHINO CHERRIES

1 RED STRAW

Method

Shake all ingredients into ice and strain into glass. Cut 5mm off a red straw and use it to join two maraschino cherries. Place one of the cherries in the glass and the other above the liquid, creating a reflection effect, and serve.

Rhett Butler

Ingredients

GLASS

285mL HI-BALL GLASS

MIXERS

30mL SOUTHERN COMFORT

5mL LIME CORDIAL

30mL ORANGE CURAÇAO

15mL LEMON JUICE

SODA WATER

CRACKED ICE

GARNISH

1 ORANGE WHEEL

Method

Build all ingredients except soda water over ice in a 285mL hi-ball glass, top up with soda water. Garnish with orange wheel and serve with straws.

Rolls Royce

Ingredients

GLASS

90mL FANCY COCKTAIL GLASS

MIXERS

30mL DRY GIN

10mL BENEDICTINE

15mL DRY VERMOUTH

15mL SWEET VERMOUTH (BIANCO)

CRACKED ICE

Method

Stir all ingredients, strain into glass, and serve.

Roman Driver

Ingredients

GLASS

140mL CHAMPAGNE SAUCER

MIXERS

30mL GALLIANO LIQUEUR

1 dash GRENADINE CORDIAL

15mL VODKA

20mL FRESH CREAM

20mL ALMOND SYRUP

CRACKED ICE

GARNISH

1 twist ORANGE RIND

Method

Shake all ingredients. Strain into champagne saucer and serve garnished with twist of orange rind.

Royal Flush

Ingredients

GLASS

250mL TUMBLER GLASS

MIXERS

30mL BRANDY

60mL GRAPEFRUIT JUICE

60mL COINTREAU

10mL GRENADINE CORDIAL

SPARKLING WHITE WINE

CRACKED ICE

Method

Shake all ingredients except sparkling wine and strain into glass, top up with wine and serve with straws.

Rum Rebellion

Ingredients

GLASS

185mL OLD FASHIONED SPIRIT GLASS

MIXERS

30mL BACARDI RUM

5mL CHERRY BRANDY

30mL BANANA LIQUEUR

75mL PINEAPPLE JUICE

1 scoop CRUSHED ICE

GARNISH

PINEAPPLE WEDGE

Method

Blend ingredients until smooth and pour into a glass. Serve garnished with pineapple wedge.

Running Hot

Ingredients

GLASS

185mL OLD FASHIONED SPIRIT GLASS

MIXERS

45mL BACARDI RUM

40mL PINEAPPLE JUICE

30mL COINTREAU

1 dash GRENADINE CORDIAL

ICE CUBES

Method

Shake all ingredients and strain over ice into glass and serve.

Russian Holiday

Ingredients

GLASS

285mL HI-BALL GLASS

MIXERS

30mL VODKA

60mL PINEAPPLE JUICE

20mL GRAND MARNIER

30mL WHIPPED CREAM (FLOAT)

CRACKED ICE

Method

Pour vodka and pineapple juice over ice into glass. Float whipped cream, add Grand Marnier and serve.

Russian Roulette

Ingredients

GLASS

BRANDY BALLOON

MIXERS

15mL GALLIANO LIQUEUR

10mL SUGAR SYRUP

15mL BANANA LIQUEUR

1/2 BANANA

15mL VODKA

15mL LEMON JUICE

30mL ORANGE JUICE

1 scoop CRUSHED ICE

GARNISH

1 STRAWBERRY

Method

Blend all ingredients until smooth. Pour into a brandy balloon to serve.

Rusty Spade

Ingredients

GLASS

140mL FANCY COCKTAIL GLASS

MIXERS

1 MANGO

30mL STRAWBERRY LIQUEUR

1 PASSIONFRUIT

FRESH CREAM

ICE CUBES

GARNISH

1 STRAWBERRY

Method

Blend all ingredients with ice. Serve garnished with strawberry fan on side of glass.

COCKTAIL RECIPES
S–Z

Sail Away

Ingredients

GLASS

145mL COCKTAIL GLASS

MIXERS

30mL MIDORI MELON LIQUEUR

30mL LIME JUICE

15mL PEACH LIQUEUR

1 dash LEMON JUICE

30mL VODKA

ICE CUBES

GARNISH

1 LIME WHEEL

Method

Shake all ingredients with ice and strain into glass. Garnish with lime wheel to serve.

Salty Dog

Ingredients

GLASS

285mL HI-BALL GLASS, SALT-FROSTED

MIXERS

30mL VODKA

30mL SUGAR SYRUP

GRAPEFRUIT JUICE

ICE CUBES

Method

Shake all ingredients and pour into glass over ice.

Comments: When drinking, don't use a straw – drink straight from the salt-frosted glass.

Sambuca Shaker

Ingredients

GLASS

WINE GLASS

MIXERS

30mL SAMBUCA

Method

Pour Sambuca into glass then light. Cup your hand entirely over the rim while it flames, creating suction. Shake the glass, place under your nose, take hand from glass to inhale the fumes, then shoot.

Comments: Everybody shakes to this latest fad. The wider the rim the easier the suction.

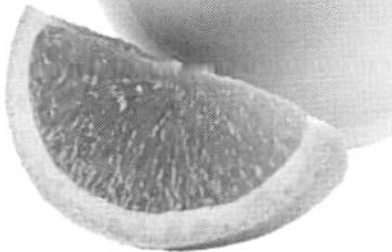

Sangria

Ingredients

GLASS

RED WINE GLASS

MIXERS

ORANGE PIECES, LIME PIECES, LEMON PIECES, STRAWBERRY PIECES SOAKED IN SUGAR SYRUP

SPANISH RED WINE

20mL COINTREAU

20mL BRANDY

20mL BACARDI RUM

Method

Pour in order.

Comments: Thinly slice orange and lime and place in bowl. Pour in sugar syrup and allow to stand for several hours. Add red wine into glass until half full and add other ingredients.

Scarlett O'Hara

Ingredients

GLASS

130mL COCKTAIL GLASS

MIXERS

30mL SOUTHERN COMFORT

30mL CRANBERRY JUICE

15mL LIME JUICE

CRACKED ICE

GARNISH

1 MARASCHINO CHERRY

1 LIME SLICE

Method

Shake all ingredients with ice and strain into glass. Garnish with maraschino cherry and lime slice.

Comments: Named after the famous character from Margaret Mitchell's epic novel 'Gone with the Wind'.

Scorpion

Ingredients

GLASS

180mL MARGARITA GLASS

MIXERS

15mL DARK RUM

15mL COGNAC

15mL SAMBUCA

15mL ORGEAT

45mL ORANGE JUICE

15mL LEMON JUICE

CRACKED ICE

GARNISH

1 LIME WHEEL

1 CHERRY

Method

Blend all ingredients with ice and pour into glass. Garnish with a lime wheel and cherry.

Comments: The trading capital of the Middle East is where this perilous animal and cocktail comes from! Like the animal this cocktail has a sting in its tail. Orgeat is an almond-flavoured non-alcoholic syrup. Amaretto may be used as a substitute.

Scotch Mist

Ingredients

GLASS

150mL OLD FASHIONED SPIRIT GLASS

MIXERS

30mL SCOTCH WHISKY

ICE CUBES

GARNISH

LEMON RIND

Method

Shake over ice and pour into glass. Garnish with lemon rind.

Screwdriver

Ingredients

GLASS

210mL OLD FASHIONED SPIRIT GLASS

MIXERS

45mL VODKA

45mL ORANGE JUICE

ICE CUBES

GARNISH

TWIST OR SPIRAL OF ORANGE RIND

Method

Build over ice. Serve garnished with orange twist.

Comments: A frequently requested mixed drink. Suitable at any time of day. The original recipe contains equal measurements of vodka and orange juice.

Variations: A Comfortable Screw is made with 30mL Vodka, 15mL Southern Comfort and topped with orange juice.

A Slow Comfortable Screw has the addition of 15mL Sloe Gin.

A Long Slow Comfortable Screw is a longer drink with more orange juice served in a 285mL Hi-Ball glass.

A Long Slow Comfortable Screw Up Against A Wall has the addition of 15mL Galliano floated.

Shirley Temple

Ingredients

GLASS

285mL HI-BALL GLASS

MIXERS

15mL GRENADINE CORDIAL

GINGER ALE OR LEMONADE

ICE CUBES

GARNISH

1 ORANGE SLICE

1/2 STRAWBERRY

Method

Pour Grenadine over ice. Top up with ginger ale or lemonade. Garnish with slice of orange and strawberry. Serve with swizzle stick and two straws.

Sidecar

Ingredients

GLASS

90mL COCKTAIL GLASS

MIXERS

30mL BRANDY

20mL COINTREAU

25mL LEMON JUICE

ICE CUBES

GARNISH

TWIST LEMON RIND

Method

Shake all ingredients with ice and strain. Serve garnished with lemon rind.

Comments: A zappy pre-dinner cocktail. The lemon juice purifies the brandy and ferments the Cointreau. Too much lemon juice will leave an acidic after-taste.

Singapore Sling

Ingredients

GLASS

285mL HI-BALL GLASS

MIXERS

30mL GIN

30mL ORANGE JUICE

30mL CHERRY BRANDY OR LIQUEUR

30mL LIME JUICE

15mL COINTREAU

30mL PINEAPPLE JUICE

dash ANGOSTURA BITTERS

15mL BENEDICTINE

ICE CUBES

GARNISH

1 ORANGE SLICE

1 MINT SPRIG

1 CHERRY

Method

Shake all ingredients with ice and pour into glass. Garnish with orange slice, mint, cherry, swizzle stick and straws.

Comments: This recipe is the original Singapore version. With its fruit juices it tastes totally different from other gin cocktails.

Slippery Nipple

Ingredients

GLASS

TALL DUTCH CORDIAL

MIXERS

30mL SAMBUCA

30mL BAILEYS IRISH CREAM

Method

Float sambuca over Baileys into glass and serve.

Snowball

Ingredients

GLASS

285mL HI-BALL GLASS

MIXERS

30mL ADVOCAAT LIQUEUR

LEMONADE

dash LIME CORDIAL

FRESH CREAM, OPTIONAL

GARNISH

1 RED CHERRY

Method

Build all ingredients over ice. Garnish with Red cherry, swizzle sticks and straws.

Comments: It's better to place ice in the glass after mixing the advocaat with lemonade before floating cream on top. The pressure will create the desired 'snowball' effect.

South Pacific

Ingredients

GLASS

285mL HI-BALL GLASS

MIXERS

30mL GIN

15mL GALLIANO LIQUEUR

LEMONADE

15mL BLUE CURAÇAO

ICE CUBES

GARNISH

1 LEMON SLICE

1 CHERRY

Method

Build gin, Galliano and lemonade over ice, then add the Blue Curaçao. Garnish with lemon slice and cherry, a swizzle stick and straws.

Comments: Australia's first gold-medal winning cocktail. Created by Gary Revell, won the World Cocktail Championships in Yugoslavia.

Soviet Cocktail

Ingredients

GLASS

90mL COCKTAIL GLASS

MIXERS

30mL VODKA

10mL DRY VERMOUTH

10mL AMONTILLADO SHERRY

ICE CUBES

GARNISH

1 twist LEMON RIND

Method

Shake all ingredients over ice and pour into glass. Garnish with a twist of lemon.

Comments: Amontillado sherry has a medium dry taste and nutty flavour. May be substituted by Amaretto.

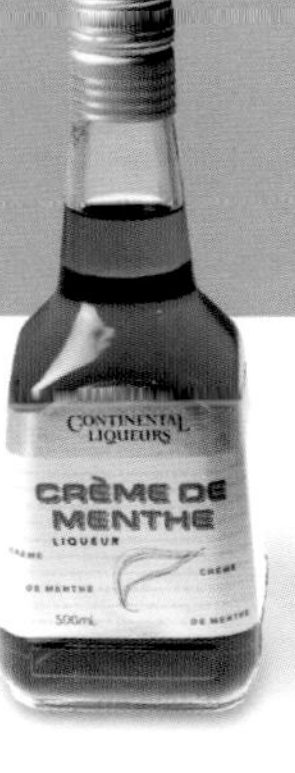

Spanish Moss

Ingredients

GLASS

150mL OLD FASHIONED SPIRIT GLASS

MIXERS

30mL CHAMBORD

10mL KAHLÚA

5mL GREEN CRÈME DE MENTHE

ICE CUBES

GARNISH

1 GREEN CHERRY

Method

Shake all ingredients with ice and strain over a cube of ice into glass. Garnish with a green cherry.

Comments: Chambord is a raspberry-flavoured liqueur from France.

Spritzer

Ingredients

GLASS

185mL WINE GLASS

MIXERS

DRY WHITE WINE

CHILLED SODA WATER

Method

Build, no ice.

Comments: 'Wet the whistle' with a responsible alternative. Most prefer the soda water dilution although you may prefer lemonade.

St Moritz

Ingredients

GLASS

150mL OLD FASHIONED SPIRIT GLASS

MIXERS

30mL SCHNAPPS

ICE CUBES

GARNISH

DOUBLE CREAM

Method

Pour into glass over ice. Float in a layer of double cream.

Comments: Traditionally this drink is made with Chambord (a raspberry-flavoured liqueur from France) instead of schnapps.

Stars and Stripes

Ingredients

GLASS

300mL FANCY COCKTAIL GLASS

MIXERS

10mL BLUE CURAÇAO

BLEND 1

30mL SOUTHERN COMFORT

30mL FRANGELICO

CRACKED ICE

BLEND 2

30mL STRAWBERRY LIQUEUR

3–4 STRAWBERRIES

CRACKED ICE

GARNISH

CHOCOLATE FLAKES

1 STRAWBERRY

Method

Pour Blue Curaçao into glass. Blend other ingredients with ice in 2 separate blenders and float in. Sprinkle chocolate flakes over top and add a strawberry and USA flag to side of glass.

Comments: Tilt the glass when pouring in the two sets of ingredients. A refreshingly super-powered alcoholic cocktail without juice.

Strawberry Blonde

Ingredients

GLASS

285mL HI-BALL GLASS

MIXERS

30mL DARK CRÈME DE CACAO

COLA

30mL FRESH CREAM

dash GRENADINE CORDIAL

ICE CUBES

GARNISH

1 RED CHERRY

Method

Pour Crème de Cacao over ice. Top up with cola. Float cream on top. Garnish with red cherry, swizzle sticks and straws.

Comments: Tasting this cocktail will reveal why 'blondes have more fun'. Placing ice in the glass after mixing the cacao with cola will support the floating cream on top. A dessert cocktail, ideal on a blind date.

Sunken Treasure

Ingredients

GLASS

90mL COCKTAIL GLASS

MIXERS

30mL GIN

15mL PEACH LIQUEUR

CHAMPAGNE

GARNISH

1 teaspoon APRICOT JAM

1 STRAWBERRY

Method

Stir gin and peach liqueur over ice, strain into glass and top up with Champagne. Place apricot jam in the bottom of glass and then push a strawberry into jam.

Comments: It is always pleasing to include innovative cocktail garnishes.

TNT

Ingredients

GLASS

90mL COCKTAIL GLASS

MIXERS

45mL BRANDY

20mL ORANGE LIQUEUR

dash PERNOD

dash ANGOSTURA BITTERS

GARNISH

ORANGE TWIST

Method

Stir all ingredients over ice and strain into glass.

Comments: A powder keg, a cocktail that will really liven up the party. Drink in moderation, as this one can really cause a 'bang'.

Tall Dutch Egg Nog

Ingredients

GLASS

300mL BEER GLASS OR MUG

MIXERS

30mL BACARDI RUM

30mL ORANGE JUICE

10mL DARK RUM

10mL ADVOCAAT

120mL MILK

CRACKED ICE

GARNISH

CINNAMON

EGG

Method

Blend all ingredients with ice and pour into glass. Garnish with a sprinkle of cinnamon and egg.

Tauris

Ingredients

GLASS

OLD FASHIONED GLASS SPIRIT GLASS

MIXERS

4 LIMES

MINT

RAW SUGAR AND SUGAR SYRUP

30mL VODKA

30mL MIDORI MELON LIQUEUR

dash CRANBERRY JUICE

ICE CUBES

Method

Muddle the limes, mint and sugar in glass. Add the remaining ingredients. Stir vigorously and serve.

Temptation

Ingredients

GLASS

140mL CHAMPAGNE SAUCER

MIXERS

60mL CANADIAN CLUB RYE WHISKEY

15mL DUBONNET

15mL PERNOD

15mL WHITE CURAÇAO

ICE CUBES

GARNISH

1 twist ORANGE RIND

Method

Stir all ingredients with ice and strain into champagne saucer. Garnish with twist of orange rind and serve.

Tennessee Sour

Ingredients

GLASS

140mL FANCY COCKTAIL

MIXERS

60mL JACK DANIEL'S TENNESSEE WHISKEY

JUICE 1/2 LEMON

1/2 teaspoon SUGAR

CRACKED ICE

SODA WATER

GARNISH

1/2 slice LEMON

1 MARASCHINO CHERRY

Method

Shake all ingredients except soda water. Strain into glass, top up with soda water. Garnish with lemon slice and cherry and serve.

Tequila Slammer

Ingredients

GLASS

185mL OLD FASHIONED SPIRIT GLASS

MIXERS

30mL TEQUILA

60mL DRY GINGER ALE

Method

Build, no ice.

Comments: A one-hit wonder - holding a coaster over the entire rim, rotate the glass clockwise on the bar 4–5 times. Lift and 'slam' the base of the glass down onto the bar, then skol in one shot. The carbonated mixer fizzes the Tequila when slammed.

Often bartenders splash in only 5–10mL of Dry Ginger Ale to aid the quick drinking process.

Tequila Sunrise

Ingredients

GLASS

285mL HI-BALL GLASS

MIXERS

30mL TEQUILA

5mL GRENADINE CORDIAL

ORANGE JUICE

GARNISH

ORANGE SLICE

Method

Build Tequila and Grenadine over ice, then top up with orange juice. Garnish with orange slice, swizzle stick and straws.

Comments: Sipping this long cool cocktail at sunrise or sunset is magnificent. To obtain the cleanest visual effect, drop the Grenadine down the inside of the glass after topping up with orange juice. Dropping Grenadine in the middle creates a fallout effect, detracting from the presentation of the cocktail. Best served with chilled, freshly squeezed oranges.

Tequila Sunrise No. 2

Ingredients

GLASS

140mL FANCY COCKTAIL GLASS

MIXERS

30mL TEQUILA

5mL LEMON JUICE

15mL GALLIANO LIQUEUR

CRACKED ICE

15mL BANANA LIQUEUR

5mL GRENADINE CORDIAL

GARNISH

1 ORANGE SLICE

2 MARASCHINO CHERRIES

Method

Shake all ingredients with ice and and strain into glass. Garnish with slice of orange and cherries to serve.

The Ripper

Ingredients

GLASS

90mL CHAMPAGNE SAUCER

MIXERS

30ml BANANA LIQUEUR

22ml PEACHTREE LIQUEUR

15ml DRY VERMOUTH

5ml BLUE CURAÇAO

15ml LEMON JUICE

ICE CUBES

GARNISH

1 LEMON WHEEL

1 MINT SPRIG

Method

Shake all ingredients and strain into glass. Garnish with lemon wheel and mint sprig.

The Time Warp

Ingredients

GLASS

140mL COCKTAIL GLASS

MIXERS

20mL MIDORI MELON LIQUEUR

15mL MALIBU

CRACKED ICE

15mL PINEAPPLE JUICE

GARNISH

5mL BLUE CURACAO

5mL RASPBERRY CORDIAL

2 CHERRIES

Method

Shake Midori, Malibu and pineapple juice with ice strain into glass. Add raspberry cordial and Blue Curaçao. Garnish with cherries and serve.

Three Sisters

Ingredients

GLASS

140mL CHAMPAGNE SAUCER

MIXERS

45mL BRANDY

1 dash GRENADINE CORDIAL

45mL GALLIANO LIQUEUR

45mL ORANGE JUICE

CRACKED ICE

GARNISH

1 ORANGE SLICE

Method

Shake all ingredients and strain into champagne saucer, garnish with orange slice and serve.

Time Out

Ingredients

GLASS

250mL TUMBLER GLASS

MIXERS

30mL BRANDY

30mL KAHLÚA

60mL ORANGE JUICE

30mL FRESH CREAM

1 PEACH, STONED

dash GRENADINE CORDIAL

CRACKED ICE

GARNISH

2 PINEAPPLE WEDGES

1 ROCKMELON SLICE

Method

Blend ingredients with ice pour into glass. Serve garnished with pineapple wedge and rockmelon.

Tom Collins

Ingredients

GLASS

285mL FOOTED HI-BALL OR TOM COLLINS GLASS

MIXERS

60mL GIN

60mL LEMON JUICE

1 teaspoon SUGAR

CRACKED ICE

SODA WATER

GARNISH

1 MARASCHINO CHERRY

1 LEMON WHEEL

Method

Pour ingredients into glass and top up with soda water. Garnish with cherry, lemon wheel and straws to serve.

Transplant

Ingredients

GLASS

285mL FOOTED HI-BALL GLASS

MIXERS

30mL BACARDI RUM

1 dash GALLIANO LIQUEUR

1 dash CRÈME DE MENTHE

CRACKED ICE

ORANGE JUICE

GARNISH

1 ORANGE SLICE

Method

Pour all alcohol into glass and top up with orange juice. Garnish with orange slice and straws to serve.

Triple Bypass

Ingredients

GLASS

90mL COCKTAIL GLASS

MIXERS

20ml CRÈME DE CASSIS

20ml WHITE CRÈME DE MENTHE

20ml CHERRY BRANDY

30ml FRESH CREAM

Method

Layer liqueur's in order then float in cream.

Tropical Ambrosia

Ingredients

GLASS

270mL FOOTED HI-BALL GLASS

MIXERS

1 MANDARIN OR ORANGE LIQUEUR

1 APPLE

150mL COCONUT MILK

15mL LEMON JUICE

30mL WHITE RUM

CRACKED ICE

GARNISH

1 APPLE SLICE

Method

Blend all ingredients with ice and pour into glass. Garnish with apple slice.

Tropical Delight

Ingredients

GLASS

140mL CHAMPAGNE SAUCER

MIXERS

30mL DARK RUM

CRACKED ICE

30mL CREAM

20mL ORANGE JUICE

GARNISH

NUTMEG

Method

Shake all ingredients and strain into champagne saucer, sprinkle with nutmeg and serve.

Tropical Paradise

Ingredients

GLASS

140mL COCKTAIL GLASS

MIXERS

45mL BACARDI RUM

5mL LEMON JUICE

45mL PEACHTREE LIQUEUR

1 slice MANGO

20mL MANGO LIQUEUR

1 dash MANGO NECTAR

CRACKED ICE

Method

Blend all ingredients with ice and pour into a glass and serve.

Turkish Delight

Ingredients

GLASS

400mL COLADA GLASS

MIXERS

30mL SABRA

5mL GRENADINE CORDIAL

15mL PARFAIT AMOUR

CRACKED ICE

30mL CREAM

120mL MILK

GARNISH

CHOCOLATE FLAKES

Method

Shake all ingredients and strain into glass. Sprinkle with chocolate flakes, add straws and serve.

V-Bomb

Ingredients

GLASS

400mL BEER GLASS

MIXERS

60mL VODKA

15mL LEMON JUICE

WHITE WINE

ICE CUBES

GARNISH

LEMON WHEEL

Method

Build over ice. Top up with white wine. Serve garnished with lemon wheel.

Vanilla Twist

Ingredients

GLASS

200mL TUMBLER GLASS

MIXERS

25mL GALLIANO VANILLA

30mL ABSOLUT CITRON

15mL COINTREAU

30mL CRANBERRY JUICE

JUICE OF 1/2 LIME

SODA WATER

ICE CUBES

GARNISH

PINEAPPLE CHUNK

Method

Shake all ingredients except soda water. Strain into ice filled glass. Top up with soda water.

Velvet Hue

Ingredients

GLASS

200mL FANCY COCKTAIL GLASS

MIXERS

30mL BRANDY

30mL TIA MARIA

30mL COINTREAU

60mL CREAM

ICE CUBES

GARNISH

1 STRAWBERRY

Method

Shake all ingredients and strain into glass. Serve garnished with strawberry.

Vermouth Cassis

Ingredients

GLASS

225mL FOOTED HI-BALL GLASS

MIXERS

90mL DRY VERMOUTH

SODA WATER

40mL CRÈME DE CASSIS

ICE CUBES

GARNISH

1 LEMON RIND

Method

Place a few ice cubes in glass along with Vermouth and Crème de Cassis. Top up with soda water and garnish with lemon rind to serve.

Virgin Maria

Ingredients

GLASS

270mL FOOTED HI-BALL GLASS

MIXERS

180mL TOMATO JUICE

dash LEMON JUICE

15mL CHILLI SAUCE

CRACKED ICE

GARNISH

CUCUMBER SLICE

CHERRY TOMATOES

Method

Blend all ingredients with ice and pour into glass. Garnish with cucumber slice, cherry tomatoes and optional decoration.

Comments: A very hot and spicy non-alcoholic drink, guaranteed to get you that way.

Virgin Mary

Ingredients

GLASS

285mL HI-BALL GLASS, SALT-FROSTED

MIXERS

150mL TOMATO JUICE

15mL LEMON JUICE

1 teaspoon WORCESTERSHIRE SAUCE

dash TABASCO SAUCE

SALT AND PEPPER TO TASTE

ICE CUBES

GARNISH

LEMON WHEEL

CELERY

Method

Blend all ingredients together, then serve in glass with extra ice, garnished with celery stalk, mint sprig and slice of lemon.

Vodka Collins

Ingredients

GLASS

285mL HI-BALL GLASS

MIXERS

30mL VODKA

CRACKED ICE

1 teaspoon SUGAR

1 slice LEMON

JUICE 1 LIME

SODA WATER

GARNISH

1 MARASCHINO CHERRY

LEMON WHEEL

Method

Shake all ingredients and strain into glass. Top up with soda water. Garnish with lemon wheel and cherry and serve with straws.

Vodkatini

Ingredients

GLASS

90mL COCKTAIL GLASS

MIXERS

30mL VODKA

CRACKED ICE

1 dash DRY SHERRY

GARNISH

1 LEMON RIND

Method

Stir all ingredients in mixing glass and strain into glass. Garnish with lemon rind and serve.

Waldorf

Ingredients

GLASS

115mL COCKTAIL GLASS

MIXERS

30mL BOURBON

5mL PERNOD

5mL SWEET VERMOUTH (ROSSO)

2 dashes ANGOSTURA BITTERS

ICE CUBES

GARNISH

ORANGE TWIST

Method

Shake all ingredients over ice and strain into glass. Serve garnished with an orange twist.

Comments: Reputed to be a cocktail from America's 'Prohibition Era' in the 1920s. The name Waldorf Astoria is one of New York's most prestigious hotels.

Wallington Special

Ingredients

GLASS

270mL FOOTED HI-BALL GLASS

MIXERS

6 STRAWBERRIES

30mL STRAWBERRY LIQUEUR

180mL PINEAPPLE JUICE

30mL VODKA

1/2 EGG WHITE

15mL SUGAR SYRUP

CRACKED ICE

GARNISH

1 STRAWBERRY

Method

Blend all ingredients with ice and pour into glass. Garnish with small strawberry on side of glass and straw.

Comments: Delicious fruity blend.

Ward

Ingredients

GLASS

90mL COCKTAIL GLASS

MIXERS

45mL CANADIAN CLUB RYE WHISKEY

15mL POWDERED SUGAR

30mL LEMON JUICE

CRACKED ICE

7mL GRENADINE CORDIAL

GARNISH

LIME SLICE

Method

Shake all ingredients with ice and strain into glass. Serve garnished with lime slice.

Water-Bubba

Ingredients

GLASS

45mL TALL DUTCH CORDIAL GLASS

MIXERS

15mL CHERRY ADVOCAAT

15mL ADVOCAAT

15mL BLUE CURACAO

Method

Pour Advocaat into Cherry Advocaat, then layer the Blue Curacao. Shoot.

Comments: The advocaat resembles an egg yolk, with veins of Cherry Advocaat. Also known as an Unborn Baby.

West Indies Yellowbird

Ingredients

GLASS

210mL FOOTED HI-BALL GLASS

MIXERS

30mL DARK RUM

15mL BANANA LIQUEUR

15mL GALLIANO LIQUEUR

45mL PINEAPPLE JUICE

45mL ORANGE JUICE

CRACKED ICE

GARNISH

PINEAPPLE WEDGE

CHERRY

TWIST ORANGE RIND

Method

Blend all ingredients with ice and pour into glass. Garnish with pineapple wedge, cherry and orange twist.

Whisky Sour

Ingredients

GLASS

140mL WINE GLASS

MIXERS

45mL SCOTCH WHISKY

30mL LEMON JUICE

15mL SUGAR SYRUP

½ EGG WHITE

CRACKED ICE

GARNISH

1 RED CHERRY

1 LEMON SLICE

Method

Shake all ingredients with ice and strain into glass. Garnish with red cherry at bottom of glass and slice of lemon on side.

Comment: A great appetiser before dinner. Shake vigorously so the egg white gives rise to a frothy head after straining. Some people prefer a 140mL cocktail glass.

Whisper

Ingredients

GLASS

290mL POCO GRANDE GLASS

MIXERS

30mL STRAWBERRY LIQUEUR

30mL MANGO LIQUEUR

30mL LIME JUICE

30mL LEMON JUICE

1 PEACH

ICE CUBES

GARNISH

1 STRAWBERRY

ORANGE WEDGES

Method

Blend all ingredients with ice and pour into glass. Serve garnished with strawberry and orange wedges.

White Lady

Ingredients

GLASS

140mL COCKTAIL GLASS

MIXERS

30mL GIN

15mL LEMON JUICE

15mL SUGAR SYRUP

½ EGG WHITE

ICE CUBES

GARNISH

twist LEMON RIND

Method

Shake all ingredients with ice and strain into glass. Garnish with a twist of lemon.

White Magic

Ingredients

GLASS

CORDIAL (LEXINGTON) GLASS

MIXERS

BITTER ALMONDS

20mL CHERRY BRANDY

20mL VANILLA ICE CREAM

Method

Pour cherry brandy onto bitter almonds in glass then float ice cream.

Widow's Kiss

Ingredients

GLASS

90mL FANCY COCKTAIL GLASS OR BEER GLASS

MIXERS

30mL CALVADOS APPLE BRANDY

10mL BENEDICTINE

10mL YELLOW CHARTREUSE

5mL ANGOSTURA BITTERS

CRACKED ICE

GARNISH

1 STRAWBERRY

Method

Shake all ingredients over ice and strain into glass. Garnish with a floating strawberry.

Witch's Kiss

Ingredients

GLASS

330mL HI-BALL GLASS

MIXERS

150mL TROPICAL FRUIT JUICE

dash LEMON JUICE

dash SUGAR SYRUP

15mL GRENADINE CORDIAL

SODA WATER

ICE CUBES

GARNISH

LEMON SLICE

Method

Shake all ingredients except soda water with ice and pour into glass. Top up with soda water. Garnish with lemon slice on side of glass. Serve with straws and other decoration.

Comments: A light tropical flavour.

Woodstock

Ingredients

GLASS

150mL OLD FASHIONED SPIRIT GLASS, SUGAR-FROSTED USING MAPLE SYRUP

MIXERS

30mL GIN

10mL LEMON JUICE

10mL MAPLE SYRUP

2 dashes ANGOSTURA BITTERS

ICE CUBES

Method

Shake all ingredients over ice and strain into glass, then add more ice cubes. Garnish with a straw.

XTC

Ingredients

GLASS

90mL COCKTAIL GLASS

MIXERS

30mL TIA MARIA

30mL STRAWBERRY LIQUEUR

30mL FRESH CREAM

CRACKED ICE

GARNISH

STRAWBERRY

THICKENED CREAM

CHOCOLATE FLAKES

Method

Shake all ingredients with ice and strain into glass. Garnish with butterflied strawberry placed on side of glass, twirl whipped cream over strawberry and sprinkle over chocolate flakes.

Comments: X-rated, tall and cute! Enjoy the ecstasy of this cocktail before you dance all night long.

Zandaria

Ingredients

GLASS

225mL COCKTAIL GLASS

MIXERS

30mL BRANDY

30mL TIA MARIA

120mL FRESH CREAM

CRACKED ICE

GARNISH

1 pinch NUTMEG

Method

Shake all ingredients with ice and strain into glass. Sprinkle with nutmeg to serve.

Zed

Ingredients

GLASS

200mL MARGARITA GLASS

MIXERS

30mL GIN

1 teaspoon SUGAR

30mL MANDARIN NAPOLEON

90mL PINEAPPLE JUICE

CRACKED ICE

GARNISH

1/2 LEMON SLICE

1 MINT SPRIG

Method

Shake all ingredients with ice and strain into glass. Garnish with mint sprig and lemon slice.

Zombie

Ingredients

GLASS

300mL FANCY HI-BALL OR COCKTAIL GLASS

MIXERS

15mL BACARDI RUM

15mL BACARDI GOLD RUM

15mL DARK RUM

15mL APRICOT BRANDY

15mL OVERPROOF DARK RUM

60mL PINEAPPLE JUICE

15mL LIME OR LEMON JUICE

5mL SUGAR SYRUP

CRACKED ICE

GARNISH

1 PINEAPPLE WEDGE

2 PINEAPPLE LEAVES

Method

Shake all ingredients with ice and pour into glass. Garnish with a pineapple wedge and leaves, swizzle stick and straws.

Zorba the Greek

Ingredients

GLASS

140mL FANCY COCKTAIL GLASS

MIXERS

60mL BACARDI RUM

30mL ORANGE JUICE

15mL OUZO

15mL GRENADINE CORDIAL

ICE CUBES

Method

Shake with ice, strain into glass and serve.

Zulu Warrior

Ingredients

GLASS

190mL FOOTED TUMBLER GLASS

MIXERS

30mL MIDORI MELON LIQUEUR

30mL RUBIS STRAWBERRY LIQUEUR

30mL LEMON JUICE

4 STRAWBERRIES

2 pieces ROCKMELON

CRACKED ICE

GARNISH

1 STRAWBERRY

1 ROCKMELON SLICE

Method

Blend all ingredients. Pour into glass. Garnish with strawberry and rockmelon slice.

Index

COMPLETE COCKTAILS

Index

COMPLETE COCKTAILS

Index

COMPLETE COCKTAILS

Index

COMPLETE COCKTAILS

Index

Index

COMPLETE COCKTAILS

Index

COMPLETE COCKTAILS

Natasha

Ingredients

GLASS

90mL COCKTAIL GLASS

MIXERS

15mL PEAR BRANDY

1 dash ORANGE BITTERS

15mL APRICOT BRANDY

15mL SWEET VERMOUTH

CRACKED ICE

GARNISH

1 MARASCHINO CHERRY

Method

Shake all ingredients and strain into glass. Garnish with cherry and serve.

Naughty Nuptial

Ingredients

GLASS

250mL FANCY COCKTAIL GLASS

MIXERS

30mL TIA MARIA

1/2 BANANA

15mL JAMAICAN RUM

60mL ORANGE JUICE

60mL PINEAPPLE JUICE

CRACKED ICE

GARNISH

1 PINEAPPLE WEDGE

PINEAPPLE LEAVES

1 CHERRY

Method

Blend all ingredients until smooth and pour into glass. Garnish with pineapple wedge, pineapple leaves and cherry, to serve.